Managing Your QuickBooks® Files – Part 1

QuickBooks® Version 2014

Dwayne J. Briscoe, President
http://www.bookkeeping-results.com

2014 Copyright

Introduction

Working and teaching hundreds of small business owners and bookkeepers throughout the years, I have learned that education is the key to success.

This material is for informational purposes only and is not intended to substitute for obtaining accounting, tax, or legal advice from a licensed professional for your particular situation. There is no liability or responsibility assumed for any errors or omissions in the content of this book, as federal and state laws and policies may change. The U.S. and Texas state tax advice contained in this book is not intended to be used for the purpose of avoiding penalties under federal or state law. Reasonable efforts have been made to furnish accurate and up-to-date information, however it is not warranted that it is accurate, complete, reliable, current, or error free. Information has been obtained from the Texas Workforce Commission, the Internal Revenue Service, the Social Security Administration, and the United States Department of Labor.

About the Author

Dwayne J. Briscoe is a Certified QuickBooks ProAdvisor® with over 15 years of experience and 12+ QuickBooks® certifications supporting businesses and individuals who utilize QuickBooks®. Since Dwayne's work in teaching QuickBooks® over the years, he has taught over 1,000 small business owners and bookkeepers through local area Small Business Development Centers, micro lenders, nonprofits, public and private instruction, local colleges, both public and private.

Managing Your QuickBooks® Files

Objective 1 - Learn how to create and develop a company file.

Objective 2 - Understand the steps for protecting a file through creating a back-up file, portable file, accountant's copy, and how to rebuild the data in the case there's an error.

Objective 3 - Learn how to determine the age of the software by release number, and how to download software updates using QuickBooks® technical support.

Objective 4 - Change preferences to match company needs, including the options to structure company data for tax purposes.

Objective 1 – Learn how to create and develop a company file.

When creating a brand new company file, there are certain pieces of information that you will need before its creation which are:

a. Company Name – this is the legal company name reflected on your tax forms, including: W-9, payroll, sales tax, and any other paperwork you intend to do use in doing business.

b. Industry - QuickBooks® has a host of industries when setting up your company file, i.e. construction, food, retail, etc. When determining this information, you may alter it depending upon what is available under their "Help Me Choose" drop-down menu.

c. Company Type – this reflects the type of company file to be set up, i.e. sole proprietorship, partnership, Limited Liability Company, Corporation, S Corporation, NonProfit, or Other/None. If you are unsure as to what type of company you are setting up, then it's best to consider Sole Proprietorship. It can be changed at a later date by an experienced QuickBooks® user, but for set-up it will not affect your file.

When loading the QuickBooks® software onto your computer, it will search for any prior copies of a company file that has been used in the past. If there are none, it will automatically ask you to consider adding a new file. If you do have a file already on the computer, it will seek to update it to the current version you have installed. Unless you're familiar with the software from prior experience, it's safest to go through the recommended settings when prompted.

The sample company file, titled sample product-based business.qbw with the Rock Castle Construction Company, located on the top of the screen.

When you are ready to create your new file, you will see a menu bar across the top of your screen, and the very first item will be **File** on the upper left hand side. When you move your cursor over the **File** button, a drop-down menu will appear with various options for you to choose from.

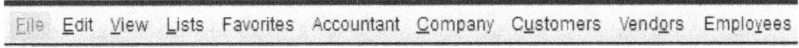

Immediately under the **File** drop-down menu, you will see **New Company** appear, which is what you choose with your left-mouse button.

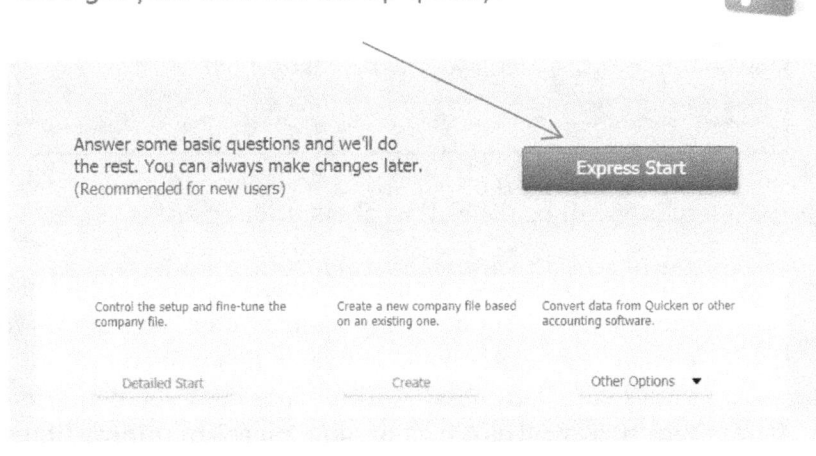

A new window will appear called the **QuickBooks® Set-Up**, and it will give you a variety of options. As we are beginning a new company file, we are going to choose the blue **Express Start** button. There are numerous pre-recorded step-by-step videos in the Help Section provided by Intuit®, the makers of QuickBooks®, to help its users should they need a more in-depth review.

When choosing Express Start, you will need the information you gathered prior to this point, your Company Name, Industry, and Company Type, which are required pieces of information as determined by the red asterisk beside each line.

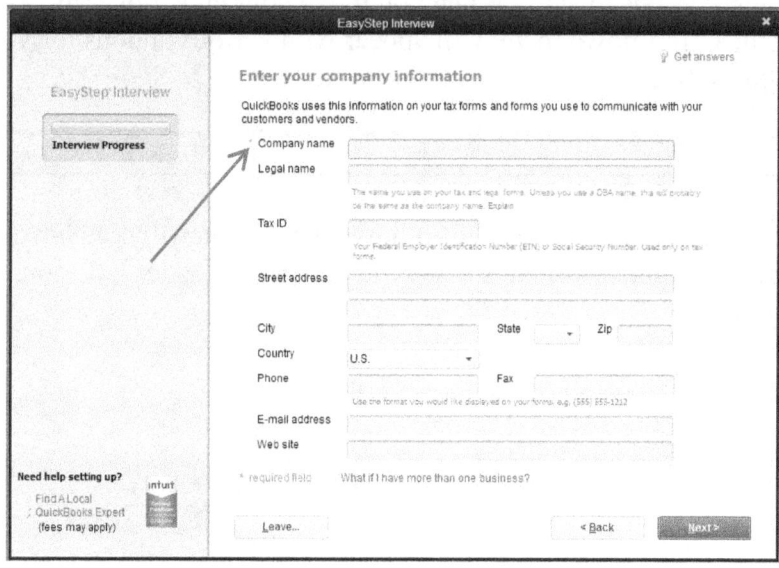

The next window will be the Tell us about your business.

  a. Line 1, enter your Company Name. If you don't have an idea of what your company name will be, you can always change it at a later date. However this will appear on your Doing Business As form, your bank account, tax return, as well as a host of other pieces of information so choose your name carefully. This is the only required field before choosing **Next**.

  b. Line 2, enter your Legal Name. Your Company Name doesn't have to be your Legal Name, however it's often easier when you are starting out with your first business. This is the name that will be noted on all of your tax forms.

c. Line 3, enter your company Tax ID. This information is not required to be entered; however it's important to consider obtaining an Employer Identification Number or EIN instead of using your own personal social security number for company filing purposes. One of the most common reasons another business, outside of the IRS, would require your Tax ID is completion of a W-9 form for tax filing purposes. If you also plan to hire independent contractors or employees, this would also be a valid option for obtaining an Employer Identification Number. If you currently do not have an EIN, your social security number will suffice.

d. Lines 4-7, Address, City, State, Zip Code, Phone, Email, Web Site. This information is usually your home/mailing address, unless you've already obtained off-site office space, and other contact information including your Phone, Email, and Web Site if you have one. Unless a line has a red asterisk next to it (i.e., Zip Code, Phone), you do need not complete the information. When you have completed your information, click the blue Next button, and QuickBooks® will create your new file at the bottom right-hand side.

The next window will be the Tell us about your business by choosing the type of Industry that your business falls into. You have a scroll-down bar on the right-hand side of your screen. From there you will choose the type of industry your business falls into.

If it's more specific than what's available you have generalized options, you can choose those options as well. The purpose is to set up a standard chart of accounts for your industry however you are not compartmentalized into just those accounts. You can add, edit, and delete as necessary.

Upon completion of your choice, you choose the blue button **Next** again. This offers you a new window, "How is your company organized?"

"Select your industry" window

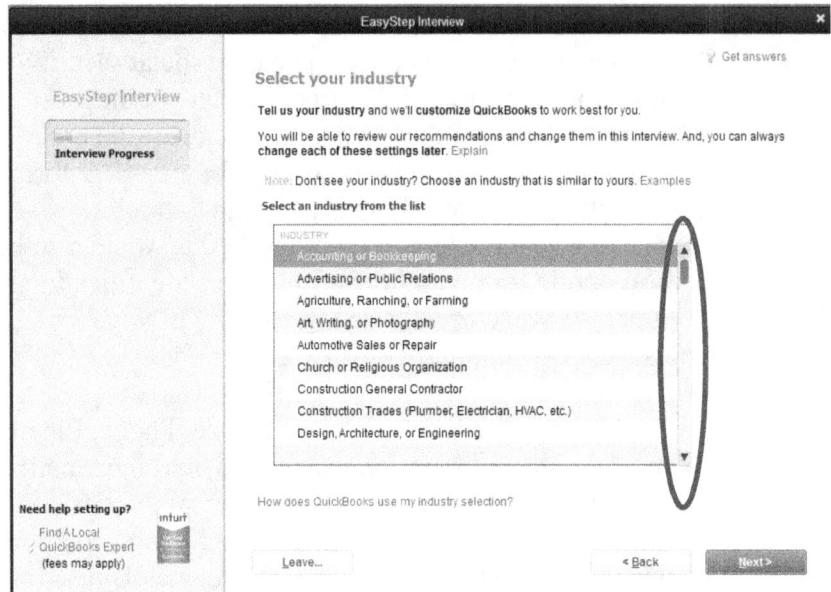

"How is your company organized" window

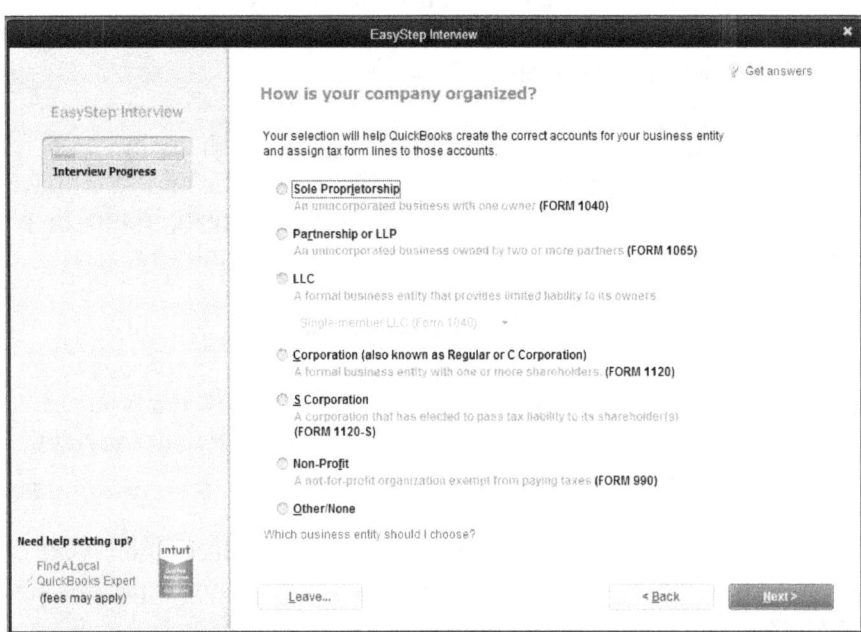

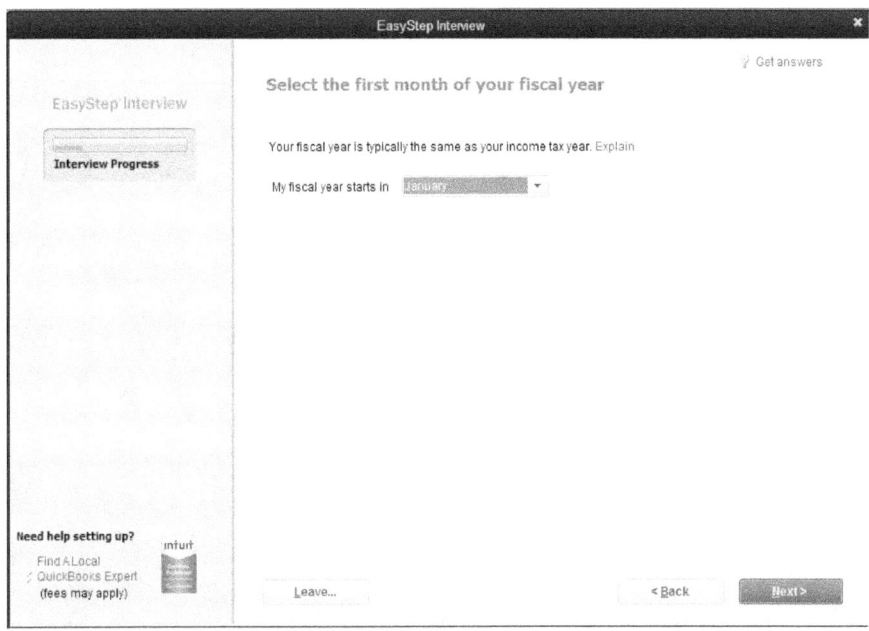

Get answers

Select the first month of your fiscal year

EasyStep Interview

Interview Progress

Your fiscal year is typically the same as your income tax year. Explain

My fiscal year starts in   January   ▼

Need help setting up?

Find A Local
QuickBooks Expert
(fees may apply)

intuit

Leave...   < Back   Next >

Next you see "**Select the first month of your fiscal year**" window, for which you decide when your company starts officially recording your business transactions. If this is the first time you're starting your business, a general consideration is to make it a calendar year (January – December), but you are not required to do so. You can begin your business in any time frame, i.e. April – March, July – June, etc. However once you choose this fiscal year and start filing taxes on your business, you are required to have IRS permission to change it in the future so be careful in your decision.

Upon completion of your choice, you choose the blue button **Next** again. This offers you a new window, "Set up your administrator password." This is an optional step, it is highly recommended if you are going to have multiple users working in your file.

QuickBooks® does not require that you use any particular length of password or type of characters in your password. You should set the password to something that is easy for you to remember, but hard for someone else to guess. You can include letters, numbers, capitalization, and special characters (like %#*). Remember that the password is case sensitive.

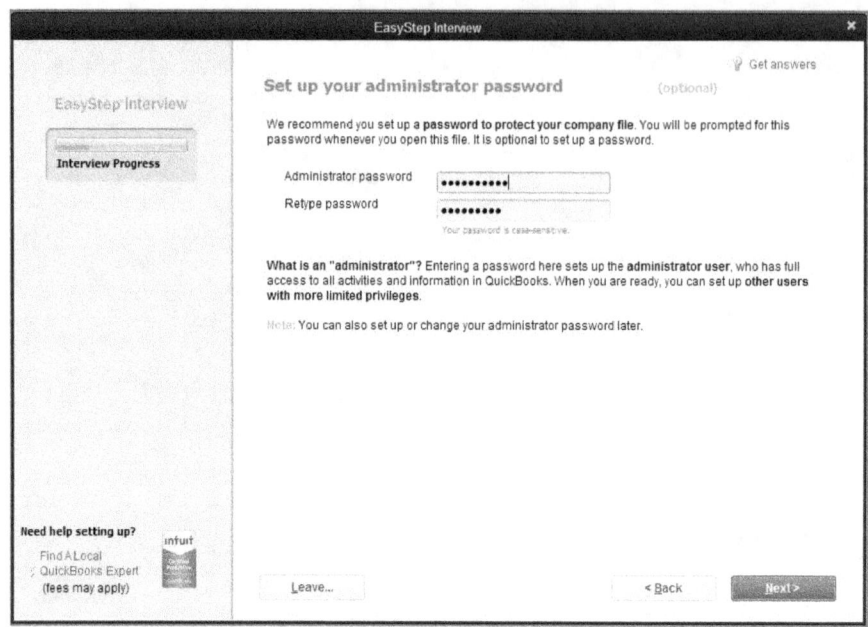

Upon completion of your password, you choose the blue button **Next** again. This offers you a new window, "Create your company file."

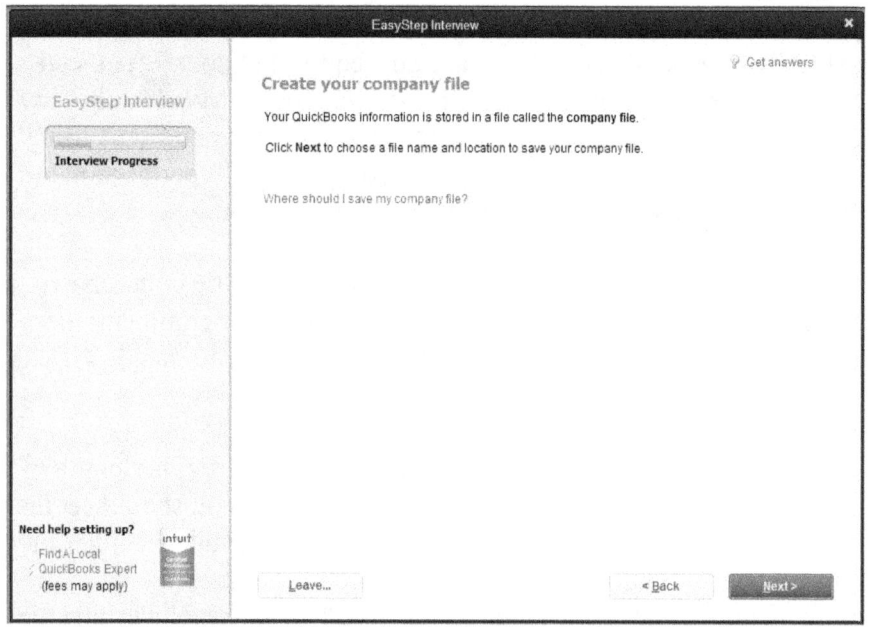

If your QuickBooks® file is going to be on just one computer, you should make sure that it is saved on the same computer as to where the software is located. You will have a default location set-up in a QuickBooks® Company file folder or choose to save it in another location. However if you are set-up in multi-user mode in Pro or Premier, it has the potential of slowing down your performance on the same computer versus loading it to a server. The computer must be on at all times though in order to allow access to others use.

If your QuickBooks file is going to be on a server shared by multiple users, you need to make sure that each computer that needs access to the QuickBooks file has the software loaded onto each PC and the file is linked to the server from each affected PC.

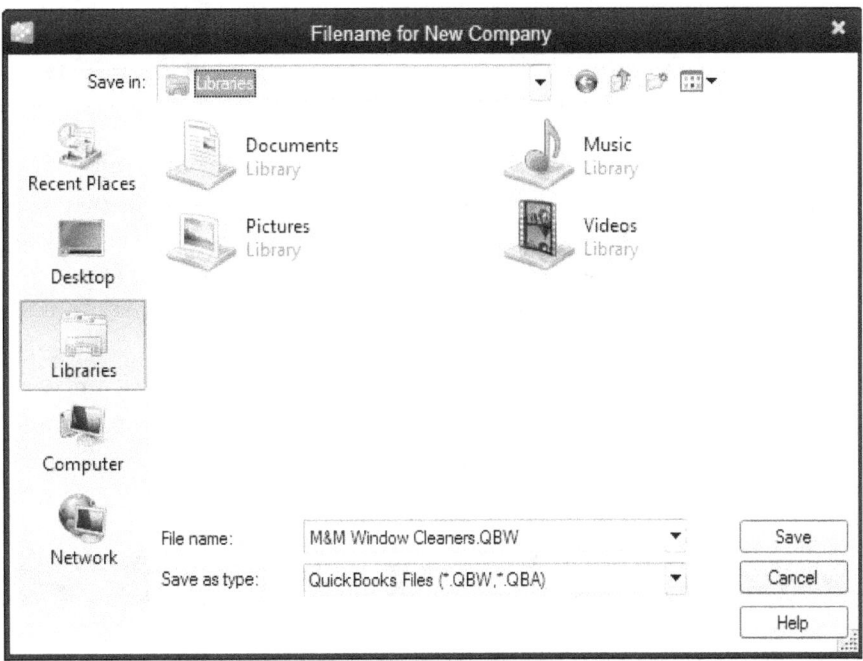

Upon completion of creating your new file you choose the location of where you want to store it and then choose the **Save** button. You will see the file extension .QBW which designates this as the working QuickBooks® file. You will then see a window pop-up and alerting you to "Creating New Company File.

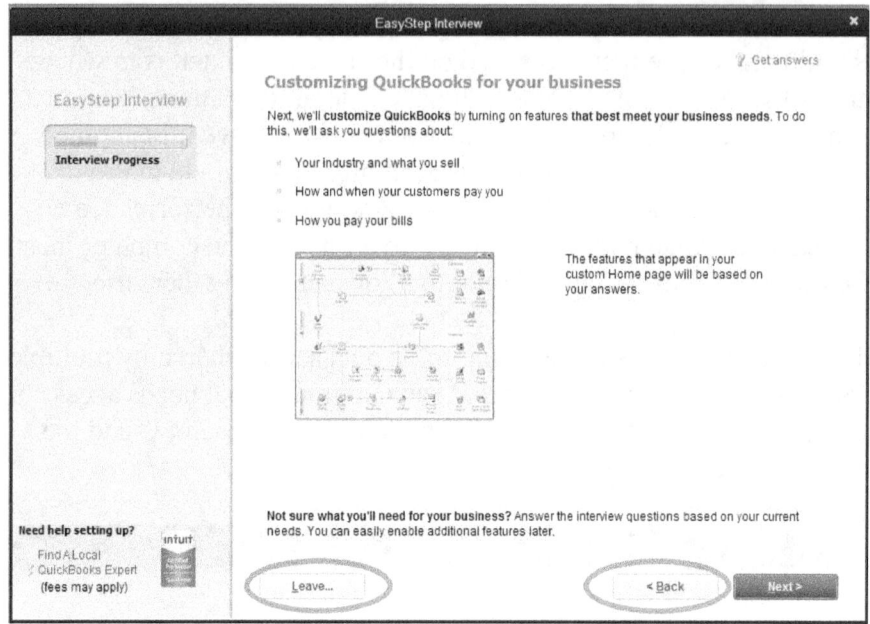

Upon creation of the new file, you will see the "**Customizing QuickBooks for your business**" guide you through the various steps in setting up the information you need to enter your business transactions. These preferences can be changed later at any time. Choose the blue button **Next** again.

Regarding the Leave button, you can always finish adding your new file at a later time. Your file has already been created, so everything completed up until this time is saved with all of your information intact.

Regarding the <Back button, it goes back one screen each time you choose it.

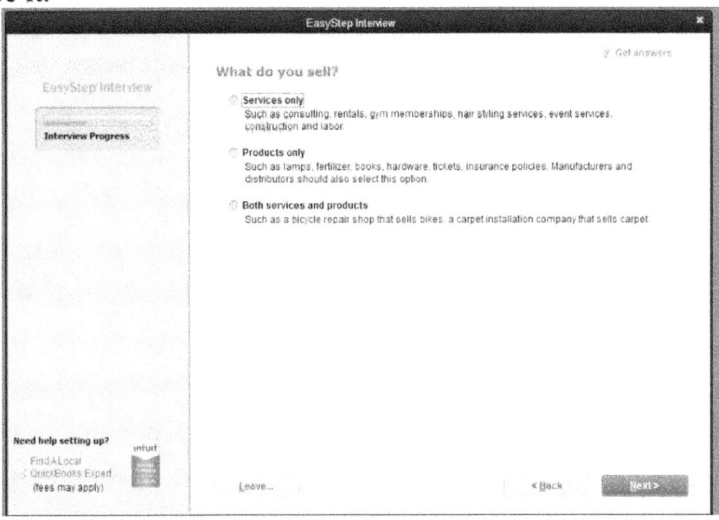

The "What do you sell" button asks you if you sell only "Services" or "Products" or "Both Services and Products." Upon completion choose the blue button **Next** again.

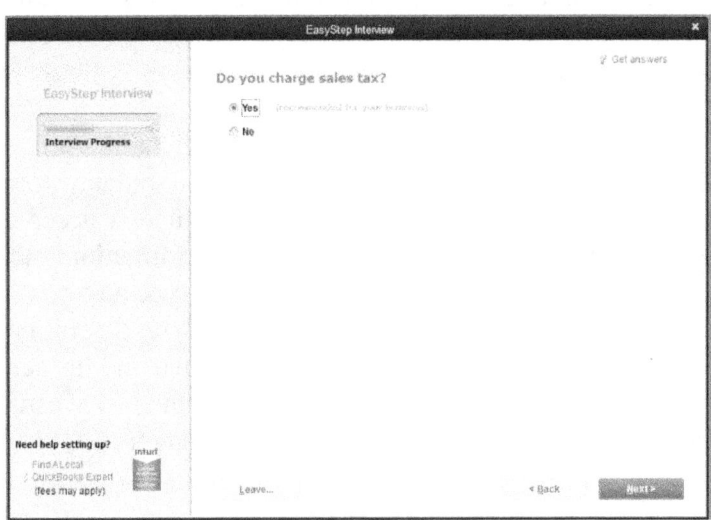

"Do you charge sales tax?" window lets you determine the set-up. You should check with your state comptroller or revenue cabinet for verification on what is and isn't required in the collection of sales tax

BEFORE you begin transacting business. Upon completion choose the blue button **Next** again.

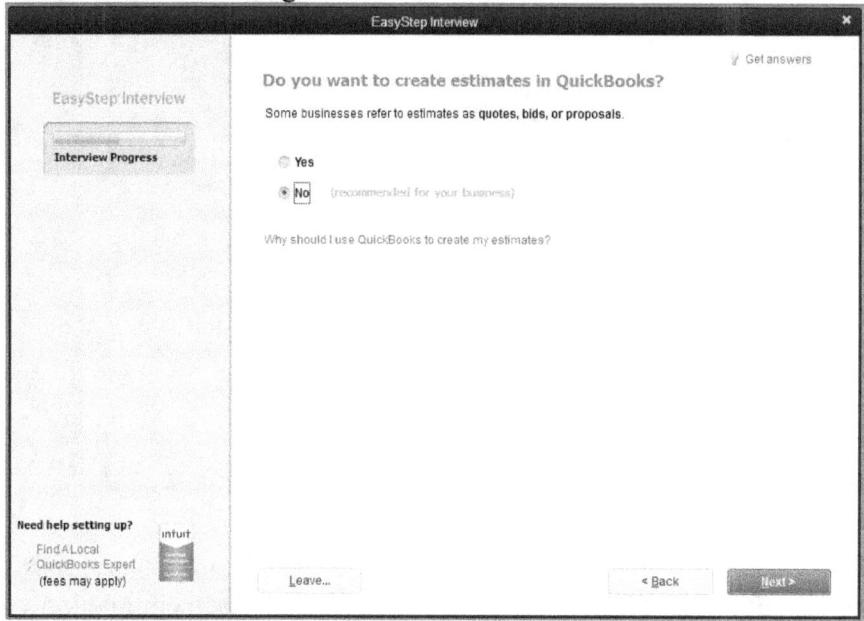

The "Do you want to create estimates in QuickBooks?" window asks you and recommends, based upon the type of industry you choose, if you want to have the option of creating Estimates.

If you provide any type of estimate or bid to a client, it's important to make sure that everything is put in writing to avoid any potential miscommunications at a later time. If your Estimate is accepted by the client/customer, you can easily import the information into an invoice or progress invoice without having to retype any information. This also offers you the opportunity to determine how close you are financially between what was quoted and the actual costs/revenue to help determine the accuracy of the initial estimate. Upon completion choose the blue button **Next** again.

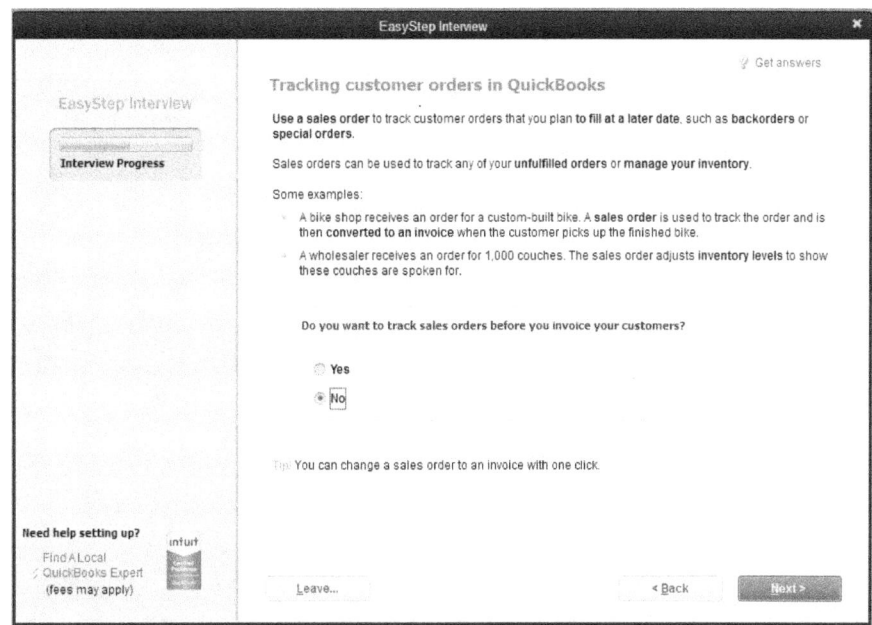

The "Tracking customer orders in QuickBooks" window asks you and recommends, based upon the type of industry you choose, if you want to offer Sales Orders to your customers.

If you provide any type of sales order to a client, it's important to make sure that everything is put in writing to avoid any potential miscommunications at a later time. Once your sales order has been filled, you can easily import the information into an invoice or progress invoice without having to retype any information. This also offers you the opportunity to take out certain items from your inventory for this order to avoid having an item shortage when you are preparing the product for sale. Upon completion choose the blue button **Next** again.

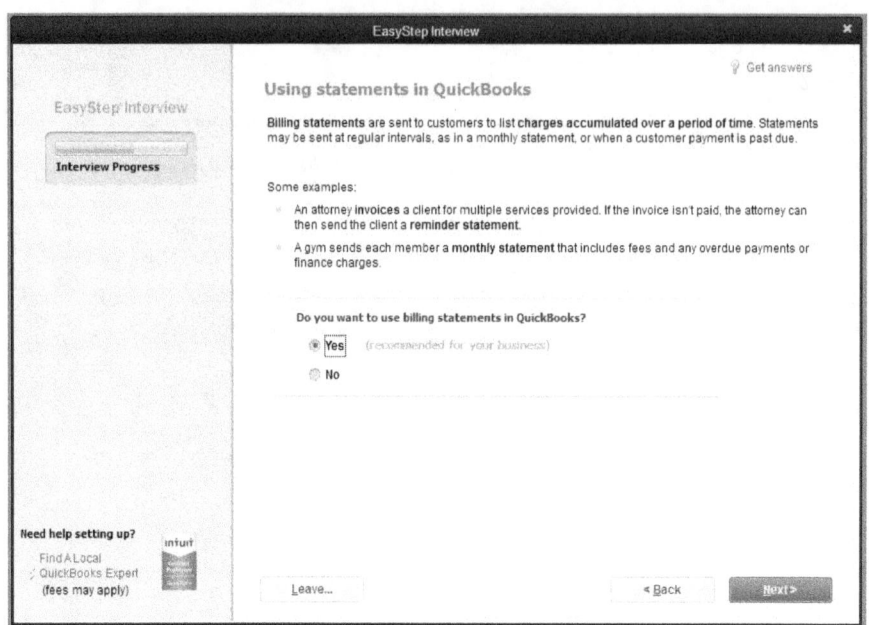

The "Using statements in QuickBooks" window asks you and recommends, based upon the type of industry you choose, if you want to offer Statements to your customers.

If you provide any type of credit for customers to pay you at a later date instead of the time of the actual sale, it's important to make sure that not just you but your customers are aware of any past due amounts which need to be collected. Upon completion choose the blue button **Next** again.

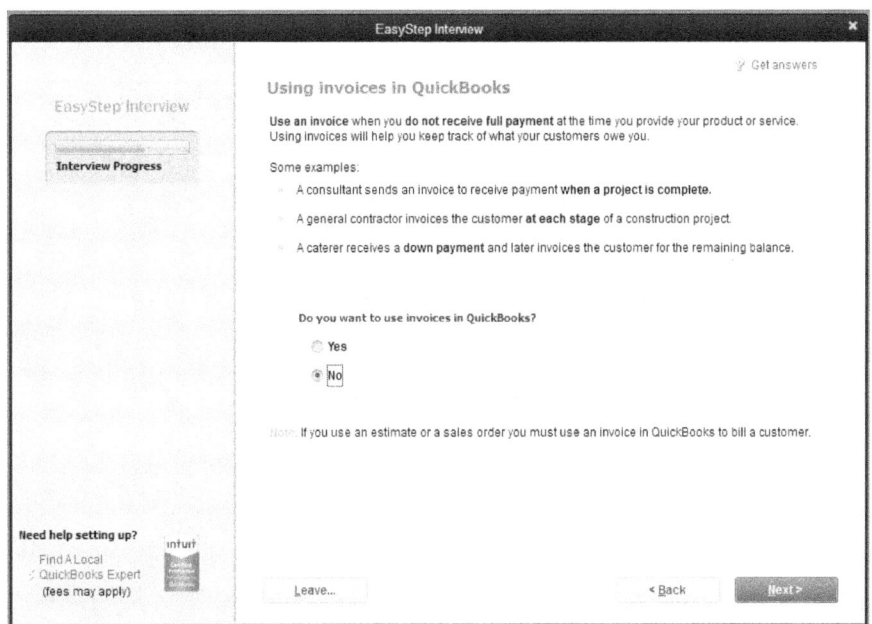

The "Using Invoices in QuickBooks" window asks you and recommends, based upon the type of industry you choose, if you want to offer Invoices to your customers.

If you choose to provide any type of credit for customers to pay you at a later date instead of the time of the actual sale, it's important to make sure that you track this information for your records, which will be tracked in your Accounts Receivable account in your Chart of Accounts.

This is a very important necessity for federal tax purposes, should you choose to file on the Accrual Basis of Accounting. Upon completion choose the blue button **Next** again.

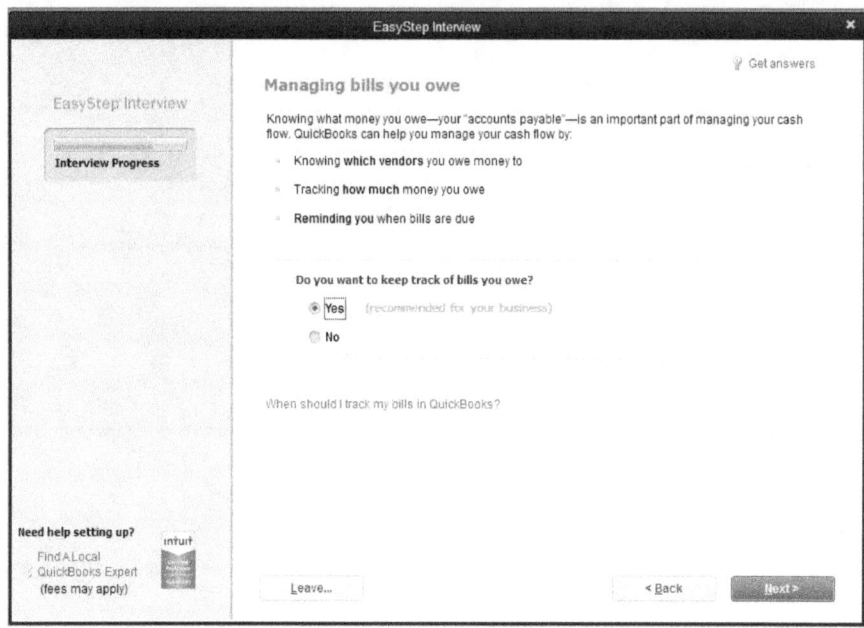

The "Managing bills you owe" window asks you and recommends, based upon the type of industry you choose, if you want to track the bills that you receive from your vendors.

If you choose to provide track your bills from your vendors for which you pay at a later date instead of the time of the actual receipt, it's important to make sure that you track this information for your records, which will be tracked in your Accounts Payable account in your Chart of Accounts.

This is a very important necessity for federal tax purposes, should you choose to file on the Accrual Basis of Accounting. Upon completion choose the blue button **Next** again.

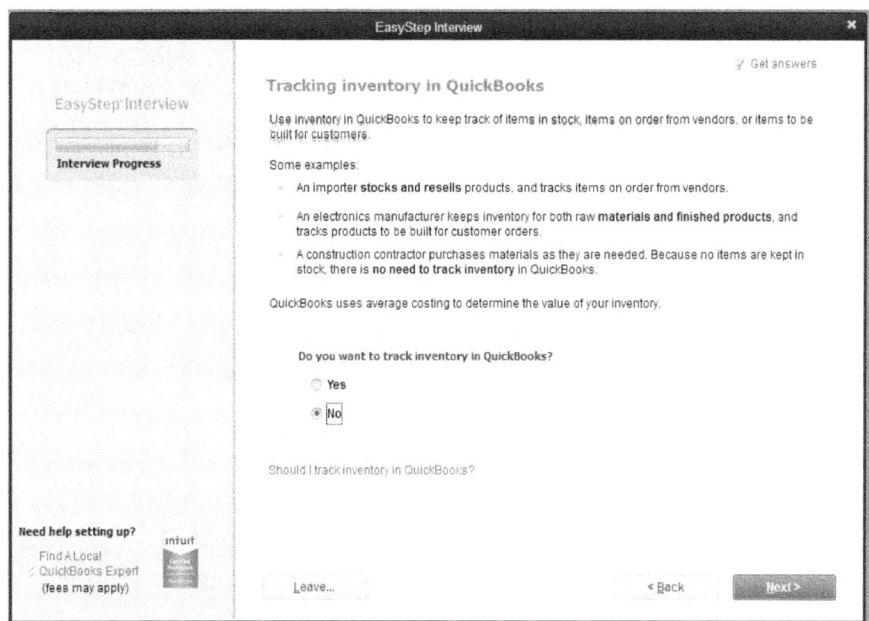

The "Tracking Inventory in QuickBooks" window asks you and recommends, based upon the type of industry you choose, if you want to track the inventory of products you sell to your customers.

It's important if you have inventory that you either process on your business premises or you are responsible for ordering products although they may not be held by a third-party. This will be tracked in your Inventory account in your Chart of Accounts.

This is a very important necessity for federal and county property tax purposes, regardless if you choose to file on the Accrual or Cash Basis of Accounting. Upon completion choose the blue button **Next** again.

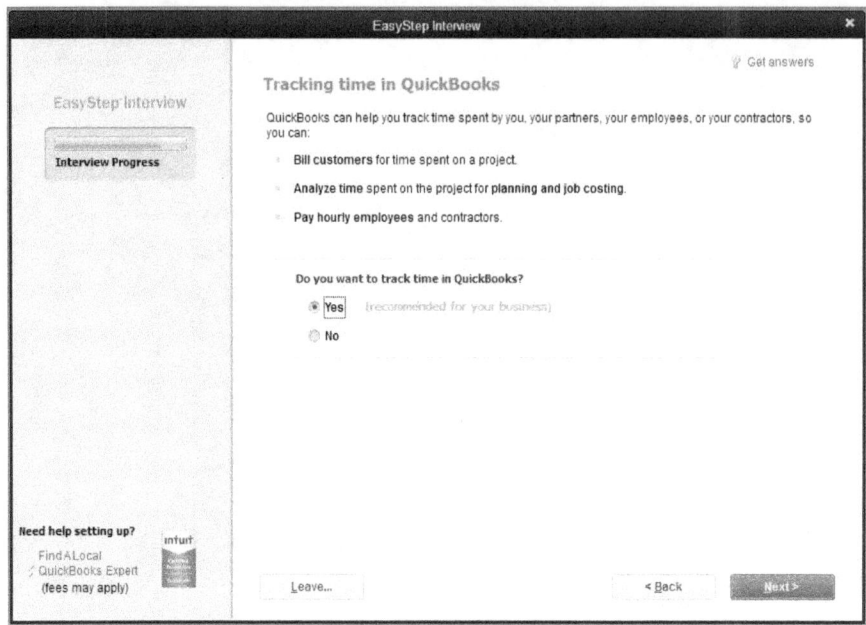

The "Tracking time in QuickBooks" window asks you and recommends, based upon the type of industry you choose, if you want to track the time you, your employees, or contractors work within your company for job costing purposes.

It's important for you to track all time associated with a project, manufacturing of a product, or any service that is provided to your customers. This allows you to prepare accurate job costing reports, as well as tracking employee and contractor time.

This is a very important necessity for job costing purposes, regardless if you choose to file on the Accrual or Cash Basis of Accounting. Upon completion choose the blue button **Next** again.

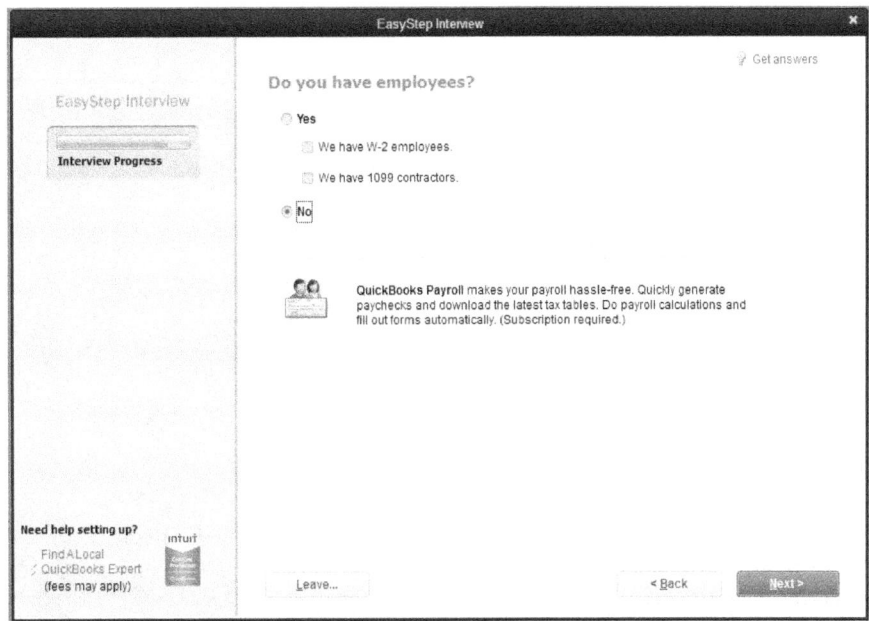

The "Do you have employees?" window asks you and recommends, based upon the type of industry you choose, if you want to track your employees time and payroll information.

If you do not have employees but independent contractors, their information is set-up as a Vendor, not an Employee. This is very important to make sure that this information is separated out between the two sections, because it could lead to misinformation on behalf of the individual(s) as well as the Internal Revenue Service. Upon completion choose the blue button **Next** again.

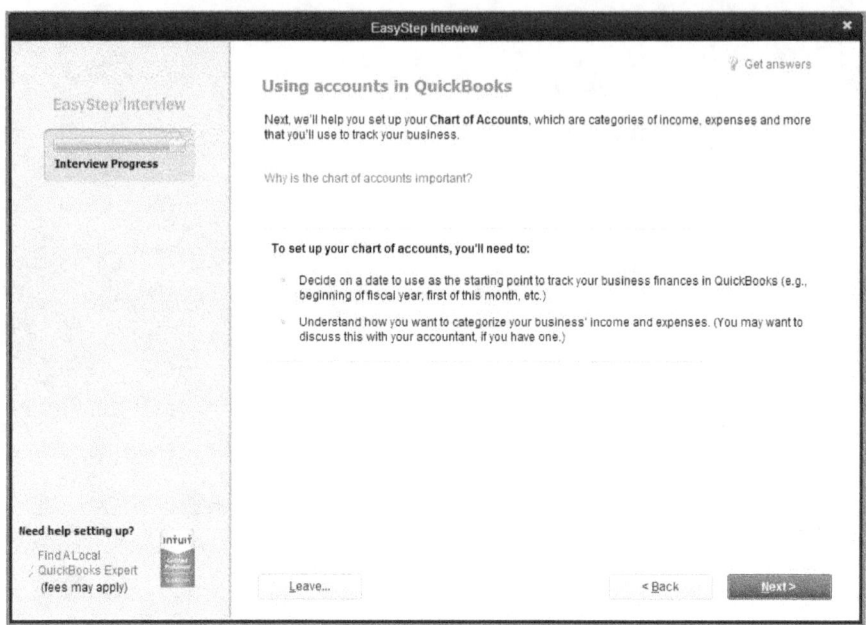

The "Using accounts in QuickBooks" window asks you to set up a Chart of Accounts, which will help you track how your income, expenses, loans, fixed assets, etc. are tracked.

As part of setting up your Chart of Accounts, you will need to determine when you want to begin tracking your finances – not what your fiscal year is. Also if you are already set-up for your business but beginning to use QuickBooks® for your own business use, then utilize the accounts noted in your tax return and speak with your tax preparer for their suggestions. Upon completion choose the blue button **Next** again.

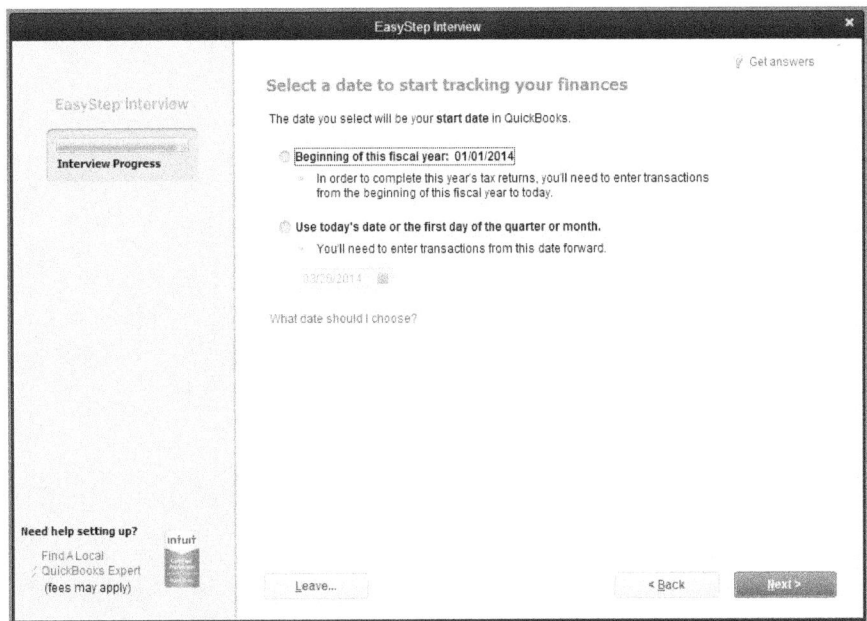

The "Select a date to start tracking your finances" window asks you to determine when you want to begin tracking your finances. It's often a question as to when you want your "start date" to be, and the answer is how much information and time you have.

The easiest option is starting from the beginning of your current fiscal year. However if you already have several hundred transactions currently, it may make sense that you use the current system you have and choose a month in the future. You may have 2 sets of information to give to your tax preparer however it's ultimately dependent upon how much time you have to enter your information.

The more information you enter, the better you're able to compare past transactions and financial reports to determine where your company has been and where it's going. Upon completion choose the blue button **Next** again.

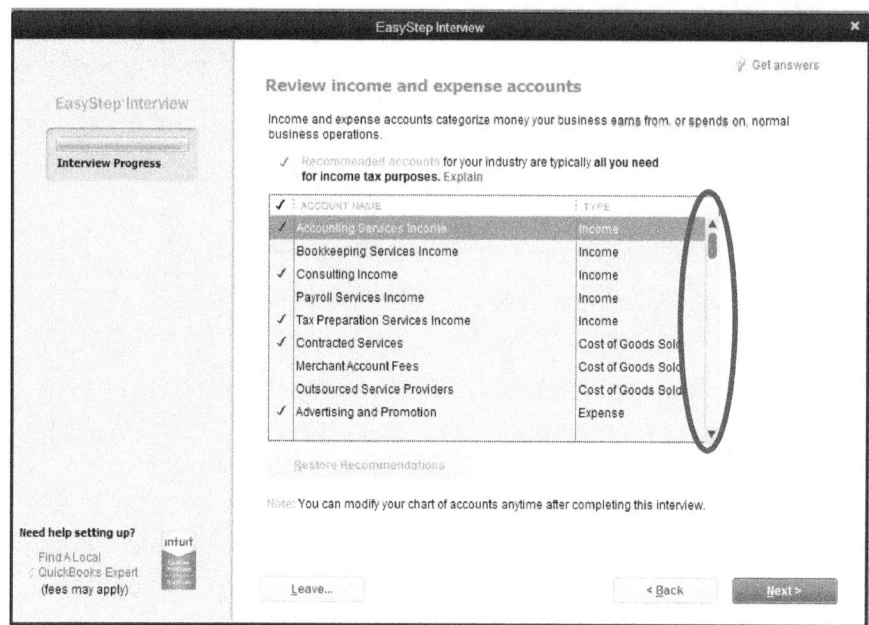

The "Review Income and expense accounts" window asks you to determine if these are the suggested accounts that you want to keep or not add. Again you are able to add, edit, and delete accounts at a later time once you start working in your file however this gives you an opportunity of reviewing what's been recommended.

You have the opportunity to scroll up and down from the scroll bar on the right-hand side of your screen, and check or uncheck each account that you want to keep. If you've already been in business, refer back to your tax return and match up the income/expense accounts listed as a guide.

The more accounts that you break-out your income and expenses into, the better you're able to know how your monies are coming in and going out. Detailed information is a valuable resource for the success of any business. Upon completion choose the blue button **Next** again.

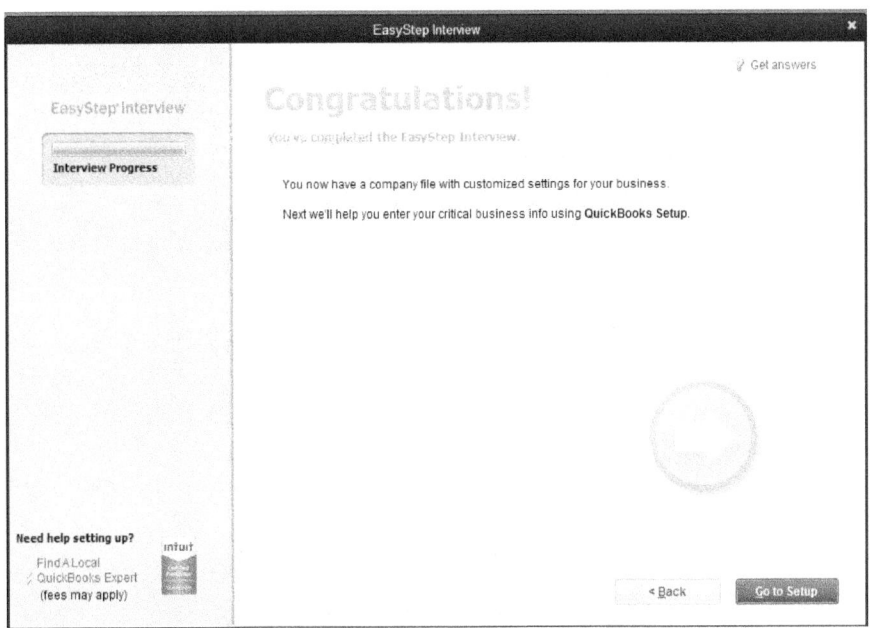

After completing all of these steps in setting up your QuickBooks file, choose the blue button **Go to Setup**. The following window will appear. In the upper right-hand corner of this screen, click on the black "x" and this window will be close. Adding your customers and other information will be discussed later.

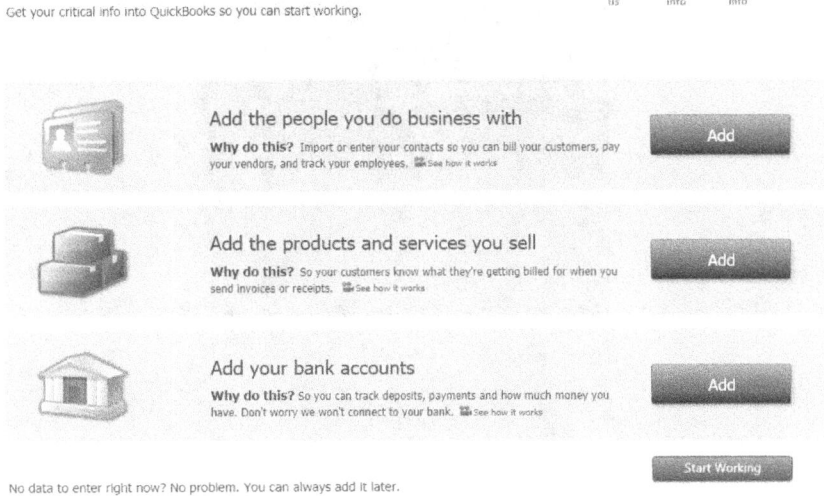

Upon completion of the new company file, you will see the Home Page in two sections. The first section on the far left-hand side, allows you to see what file you're using, as well as numerous other shortcuts to navigate through QuickBooks®.

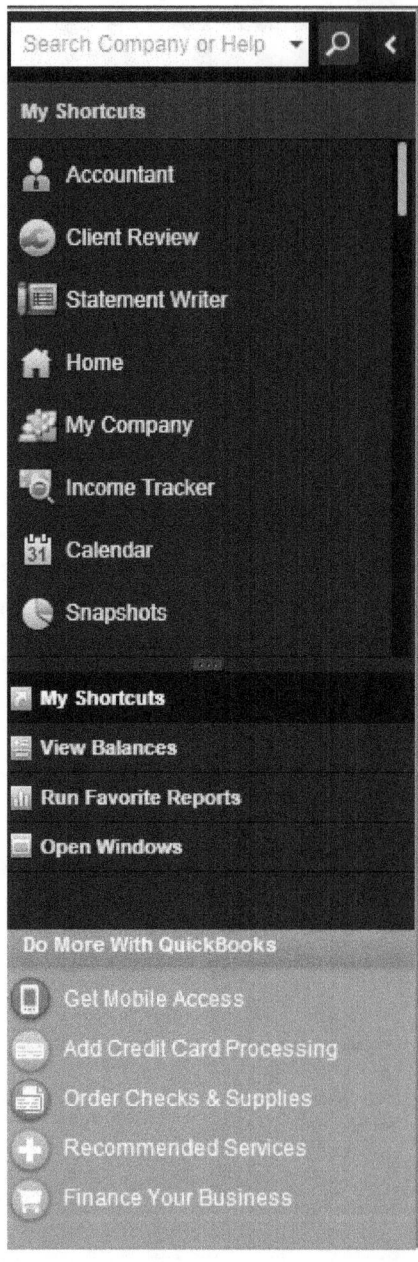

The second section on the far right-hand side allows you to see numerous other shortcuts to navigate through QuickBooks® and is referred to as your Home Page as seen below.

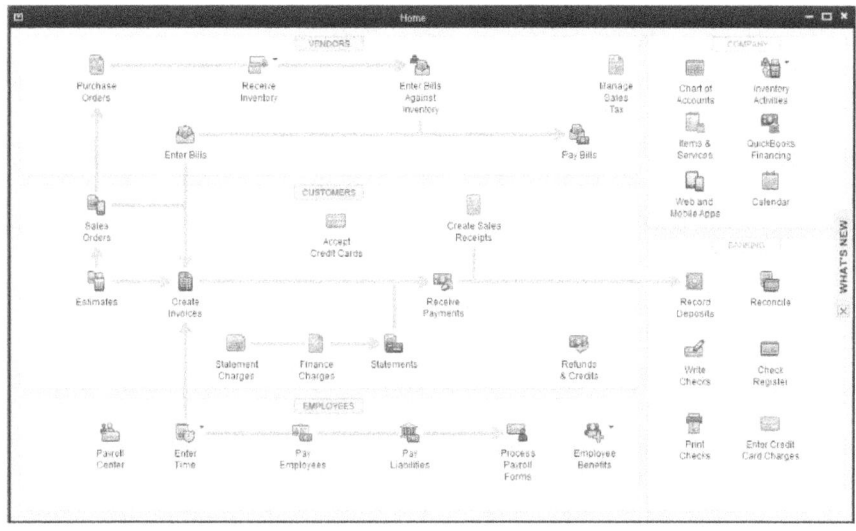

Exercises (Answer Key at the End of the Training Manual)

1.   What three items of information are required when beginning your company set-up?

        _____

        _____

        _____

2.   Name two tax forms which require your legal company name:

        _____

        _____

Objective 2 – Understand the steps for protecting a file through creating a back-up file, portable file, accountant's copy, and how to rebuild the data in the case there's an error.

It's been estimated that 70% of businesses that fail as a result of a major data loss, do so because they did not have a proper back-up plan in place. QuickBooks® allows you the opportunity of either backing-up the information directly or they offer an on-line back-up service, tied to your company for a monthly fee for each file.

Retrieving the Sample Company File

We are going to use the sample company file (Rock Castle Construction) provided by QuickBooks® for the remainder of this module. To find the file, go to your start button on the bottom left-hand side, and when you click on it, you'll see a box that says *Search programs and files* with a magnifying glass next to it. It may look different depending upon the version of Windows® you're using on your computer.

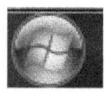

The file that you're searching for is

sample_product-based business.qbw

When you've found this file, move your cursor over the file and double-click it. This will open your QuickBooks® software and the sample company file, Rock Castle Construction. There will be a window that appears noting that this is a sample file and click the blue OK button. When it opens, you'll see at the top, Sample Rock Castle Construction, which identifies your file.

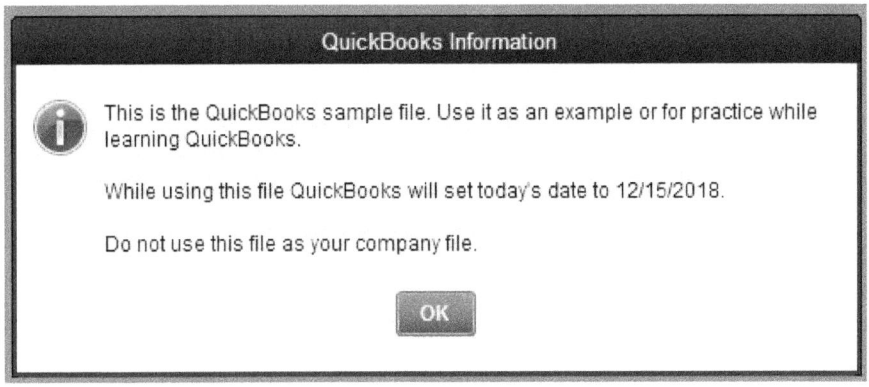

QuickBooks Information

This is the QuickBooks sample file. Use it as an example or for practice while learning QuickBooks.

While using this file QuickBooks will set today's date to 12/15/2018.

Do not use this file as your company file.

OK

Sample Rock Castle Construction - QuickBooks Accountant 2014

Backing-up the Sample Company File

When backing up your information personally, make sure that you have a flash drive or CD onto which you can download your company information. Below are the steps for making your personal back-up:

a. Click on File in the top left corner of your screen

b. Scroll your cursor down, to Create Backup...

c. Choose Local Backup, and then click the Next button

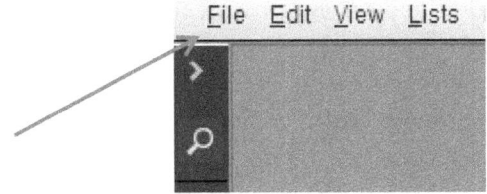

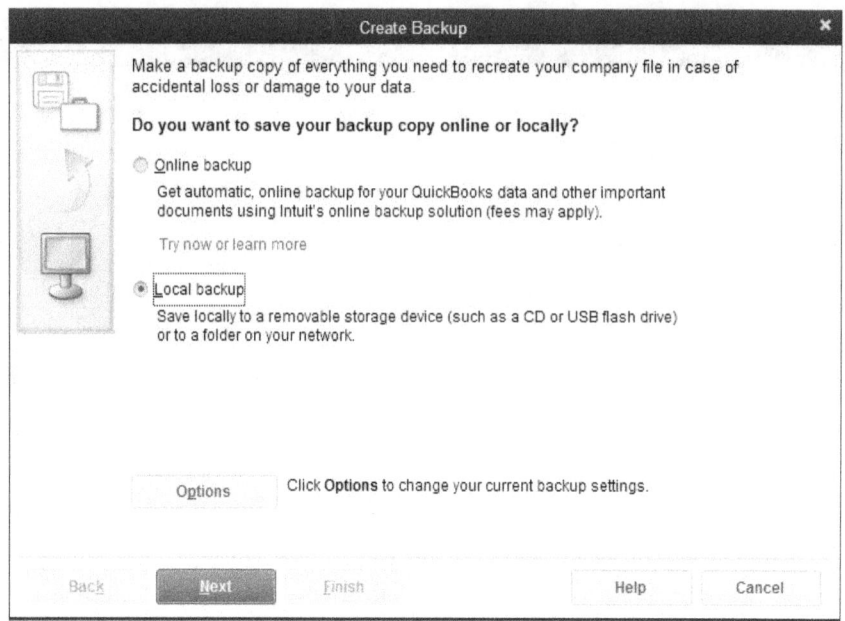

A Backup Options window will appear which will set up your default options for your manual and automatic backups.

Local Backup

a. Line 1 – When selecting where your files are backed up, you will choose the Browse button or type in the drive where your flash drive or CD is located.

b. Line 2 – Add the date and time of the backup to the file name, allows you to see the last date/time your information was received. If there is a situation to which you have eliminated information and need to go back for a specific date, this is very helpful.

c. Line 3 – Limit the number of backup copies in this folder, allows you to have up to 99 copies of your file.

Online and Local Backup

d. Line 4 – Remind me to back up when I close my file, allows you to have up to 99 times before a reminder will ask you to back up your file. If you do not have a regular routine or a continuous back-up server available where your file is located, it's important to consider having this reminder to avoid any potential data loss.

Verification

The purpose of Verification is to allow QuickBooks® to do a diagnostic test to determine that the data is not corrupted. There are 3 options – Complete verification, Quicker verification, and No verification. Performing a Complete verification is important to allow you to make sure that your file is kept up-to-date in diagnosing any potential problems before they happen.

When you've made your choices, QuickBooks® will save those options and when making future backups and perform faster.

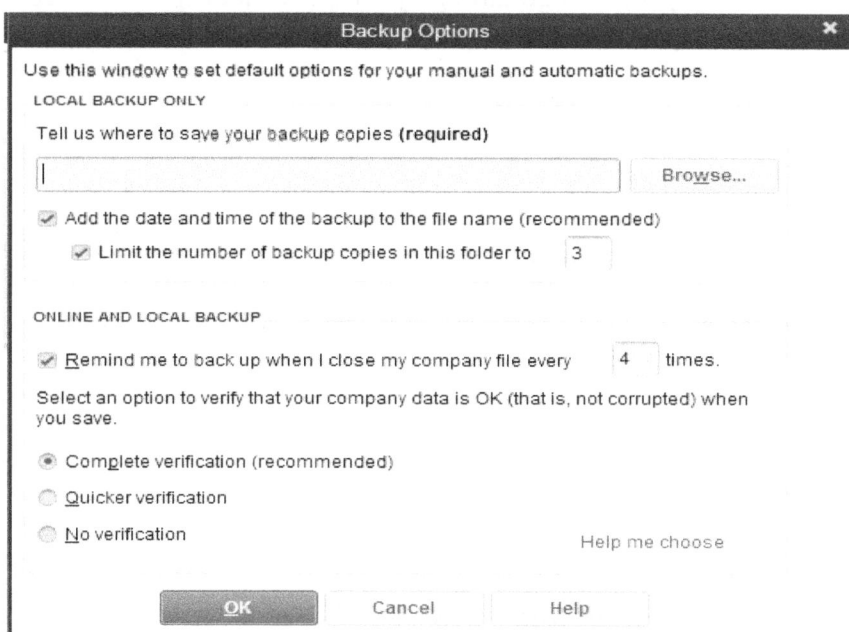

File Errors

Errors in company files can occur at any time, and there are many options available to handle these issues without contacting QuickBooks® support.

Rebuild Data
If an error occurs and your QuickBooks® file requires you to Rebuild Data, it is trying to fix the file on its own through its own diagnostic tools. Do not perform a Rebuild unless QuickBooks® specifically asks for it, from these following steps:

    a. Choose File

    b. Choose Utilities

    c. Choose Rebuild Data

        1. You are asked to make a copy of the file as a precaution.

        2. You will go through your Local Backup steps as you have previously done, and upon completion of the backup QuickBooks® will perform the Rebuild.

        3. If there are no problems with the data file, QuickBooks® will let you know. If it cannot perform Rebuild, then it's recommended you try the process again. After a **second and third try** if there is no resolution to your problem, this is the recommended time to contact Quickbooks® Technical Support.

Creating a Portable Company File

a. Click on File in the top left corner of your screen

b. Scroll your cursor down, to "Create A Copy"... (the seventh item from the top)

c. The next screen will appear, and choose Portable company file, and then click the Next button

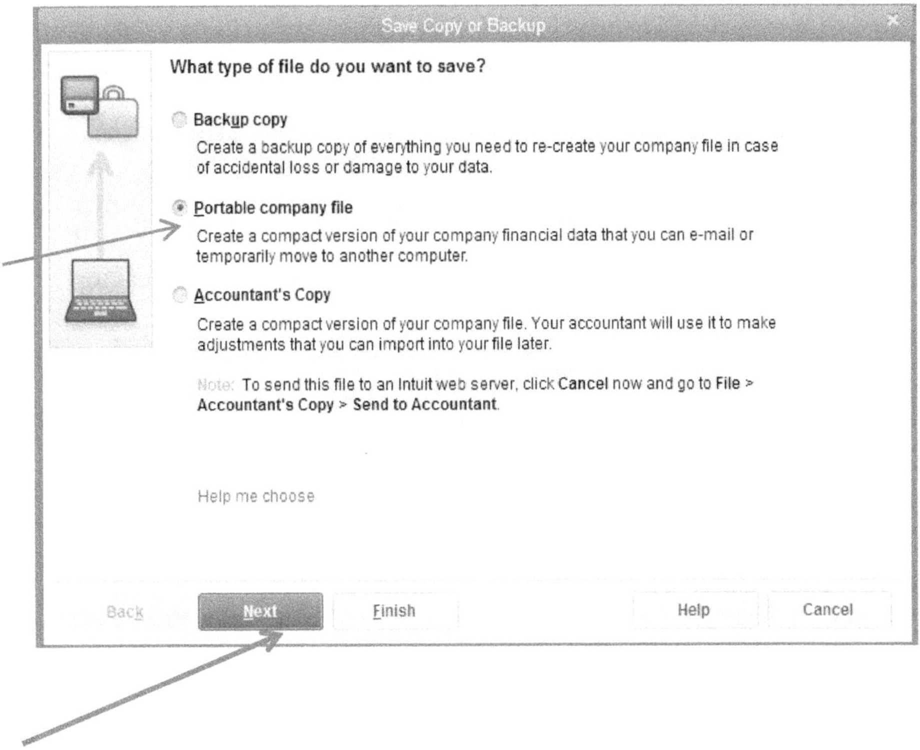

Save Copy or Backup

What type of file do you want to save?

○ Backup copy
Create a backup copy of everything you need to re-create your company file in case of accidental loss or damage to your data.

● Portable company file
Create a compact version of your company financial data that you can e-mail or temporarily move to another computer.

○ Accountant's Copy
Create a compact version of your company file. Your accountant will use it to make adjustments that you can import into your file later.

Note: To send this file to an Intuit web server, click Cancel now and go to File > Accountant's Copy > Send to Accountant.

Help me choose

Back | Next | Finish | Help | Cancel

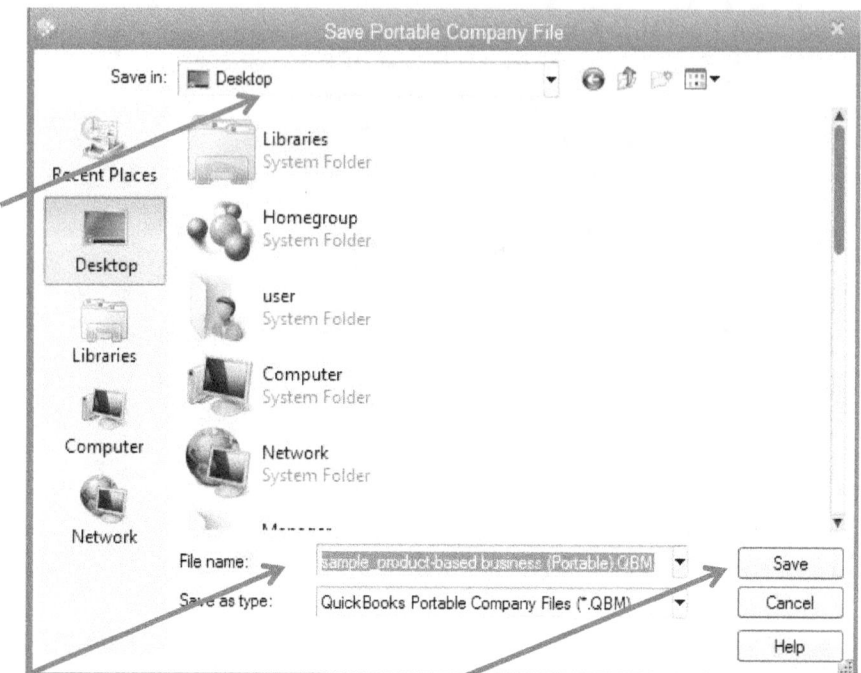

You should have the above screen appear. The first arrow shows "Save Portable Company File" at the top. The second arrow shows you the Desktop of your computer Screen. The third arrow shows "File Name." The fourth arrow is for the save, for which you will choose that button. It's always best to save the file to the Desktop because it's easier to locate.

When you choose save, the following window will appear, and you will choose the OK button and QuickBooks® will save a copy of the portable file to your Desktop.

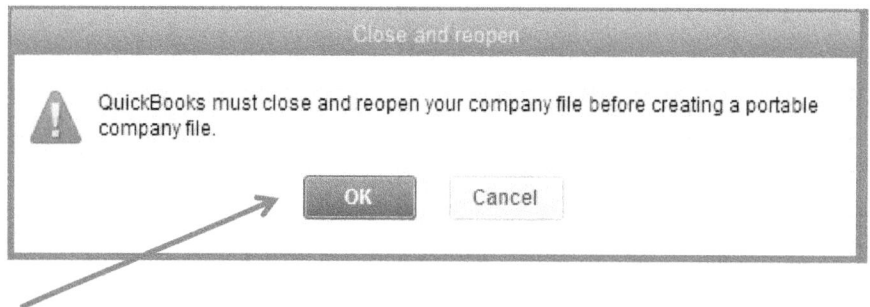

When your file has been saved, the window above will appear. Click the OK button and then the following screen will appear and then choose the OK button.

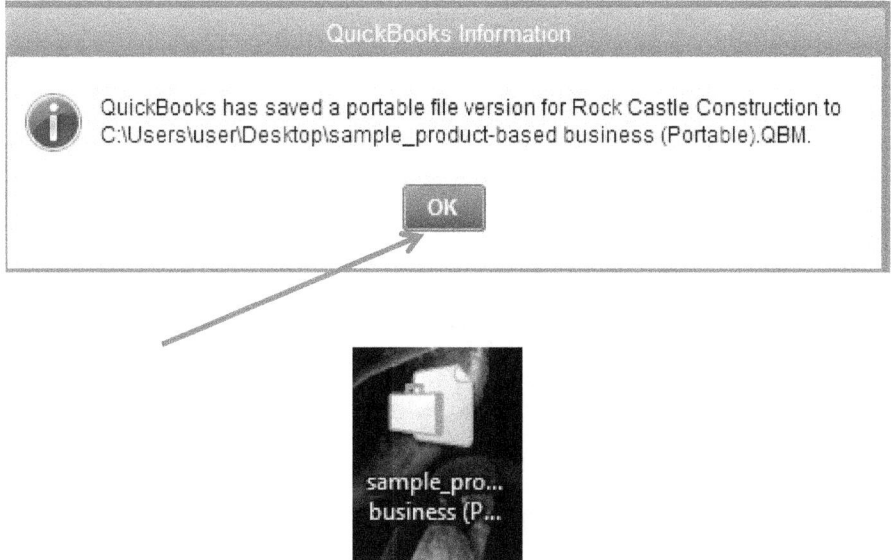

You should then see the copy of your "sample products business" portable file on your Desktop. From there, you can send an e-mail and attach this file to it.

Creating an Accountant's Copy

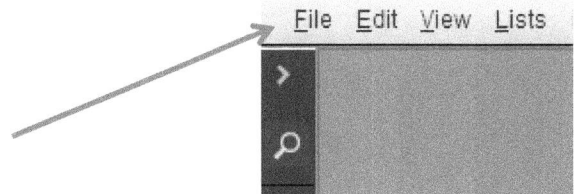

a. Click on File in the top left corner of your screen

b. Scroll your cursor down, to Create A Copy… (the seventh item from the top)

c. The next screen will appear, and choose Accountant's Copy, and then click the Next button

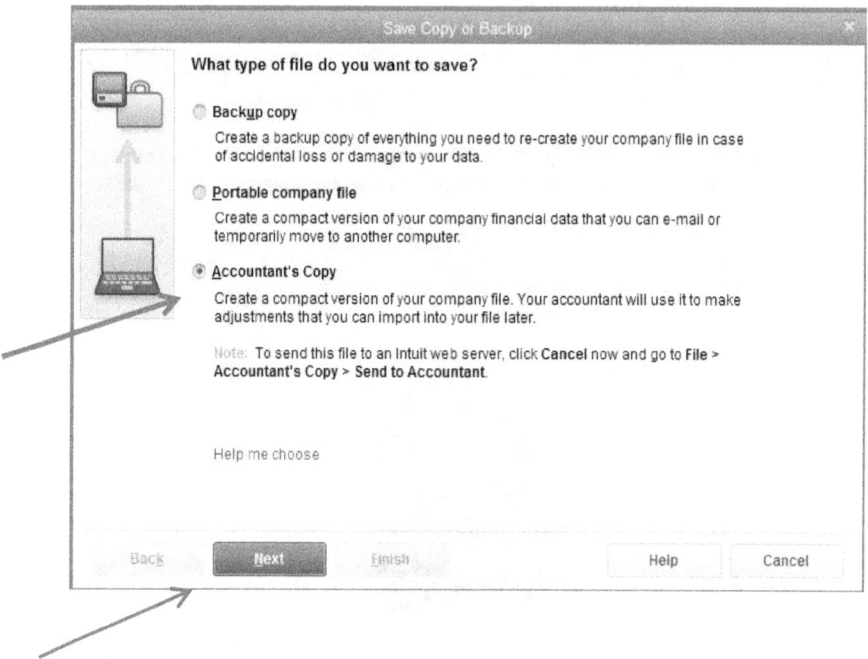

Because this is a sample company file, we are unable to create an Accountant's Copy however another sample file will be used for training purposes in this section.

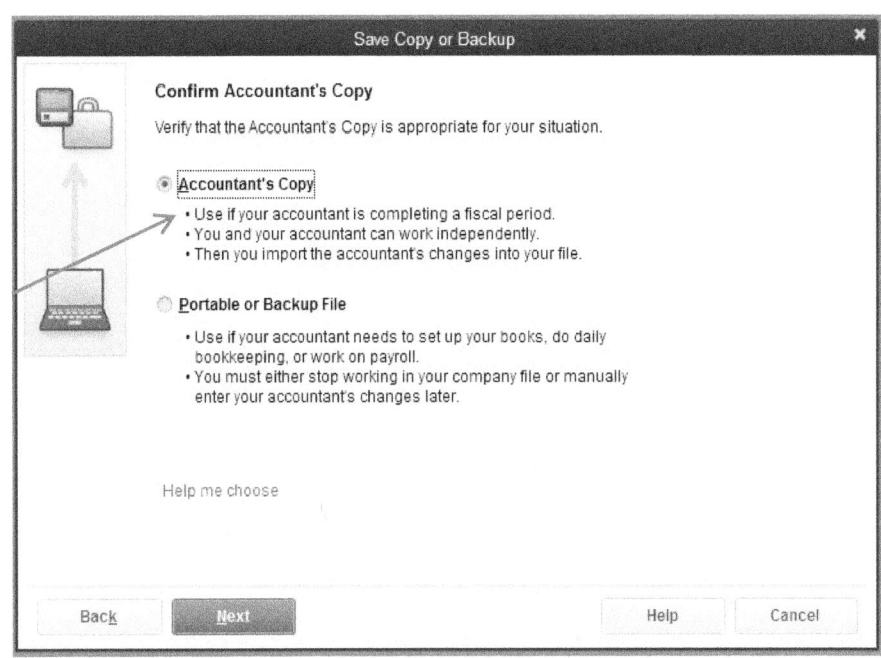

You will be asked again to confirm that you are requesting to create an Accountant's copy, and then you will choose the Next button again.

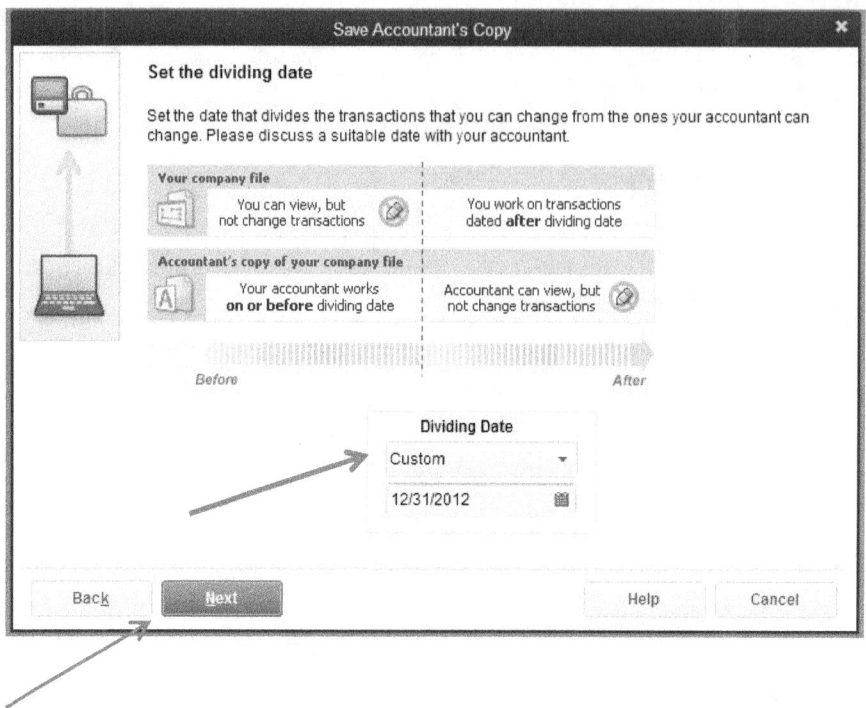

The window above will ask you to set up a dividing date. When you choose Custom from your drop-down menu, with the dividing date of 12/31/2012 (year-end fiscal year date), you can require that the Accountant make changes any time before that date and you are allowed to make changes after that date without preventing you from not working in the file.

You also have the option of choosing from your drop-down menu: End of Last Month, 2 Weeks Ago, and 4 Weeks Ago. When you choose the date that you want, choose the Next button. If your accountant makes changes either on a weekly, monthly, or only annual basis, this will be the determining factor in choosing the date that you will choose.

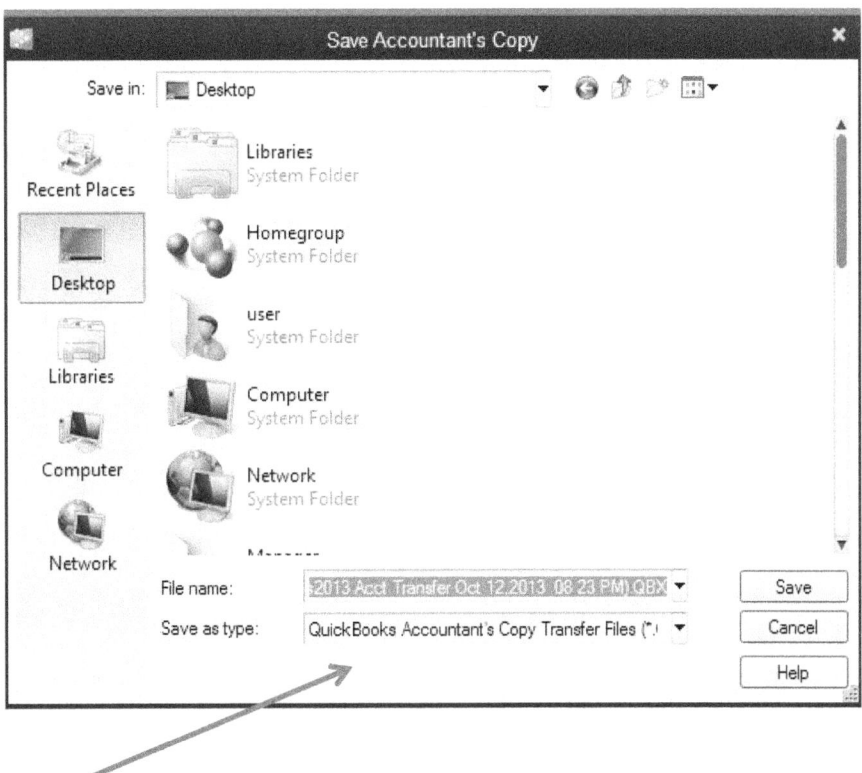

The screen demonstrates that you want to save the Accountant's Copy to the Desktop, showing the date and time, with the file extension QBX. Choose the Save button and the following screen window will appear.

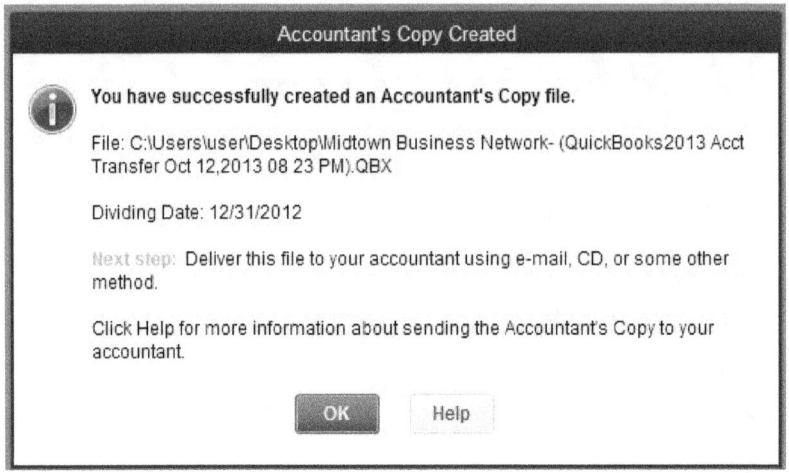

Exercises (Answer Key at the End of the Training Manual)

1.   What percentages of businesses fail from a major data loss?

        _____%

2.   How many types of verification are there and what is the recommended option?

        _____ (#)   _____
              (type of verification)

Objective 3 – Learn how to determine by release number, and how to download software updates using QuickBooks® technical support.

Technical Errors

Periodically there will be unusual error messages with a specific number. The QuickBooks® Technical Support Team developed a page specifically to help troubleshoot your problems without having to contact Support, as noted from the web site below.

http://support.quickbooks.intuit.com/support/default.aspx

Under the Search Button towards the top of the page, you can seek out specific questions and/or specific error codes, and if it's within the search engine, it will provide you with the steps to resolving the problem. This option is not a catch-all for every problems, but it allows you the opportunity to hopefully resolve the issue on your own.

When you click on your F2 key, a Product Information window will come open with all of your information. At the very top of the window in this example, it will give you the Product, i.e. QuickBooks® Accountant 2014, Release R5P. This information tells the support staff that you are working with the 2014 Accountant's version, and you have updated your patches through Release 5P.

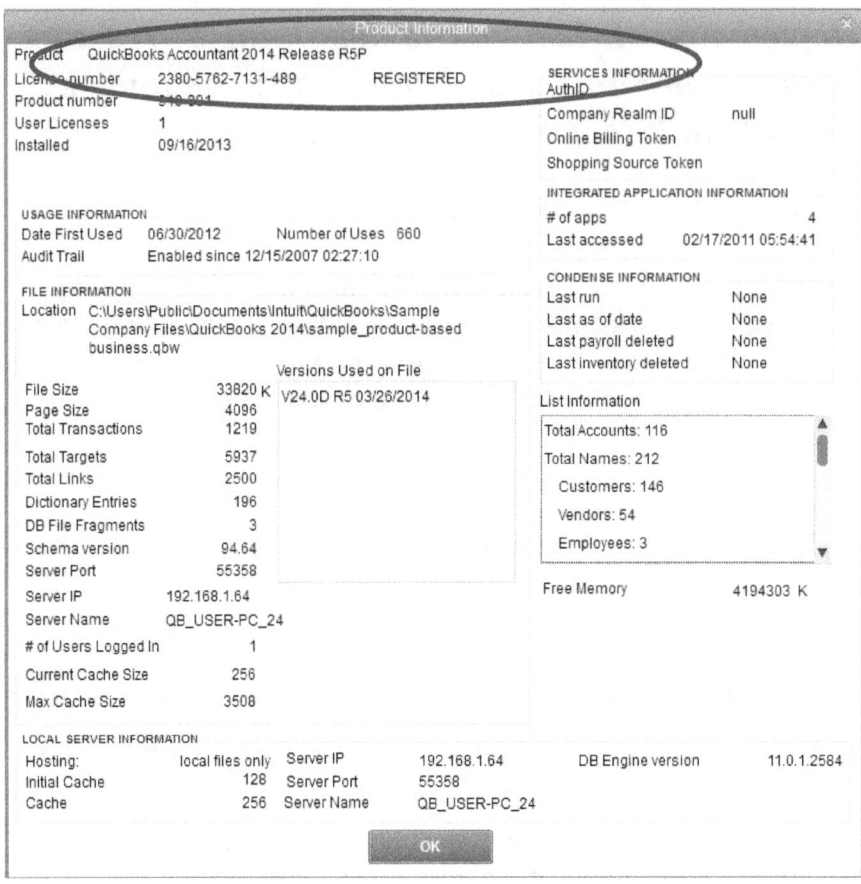

Often people will be afraid to update your QuickBooks® if a window pops open when opening the file, asking if you would like to update your file. It's important to always update your information, because the patches help prevent future issues with the software.

You need to see your edition and version, i.e. Pro, Premiere, Enterprise, or Accountant, and the year, along with what Release you have on your own individual copy of QuickBooks®. Then choose the Downloads & Updates section.

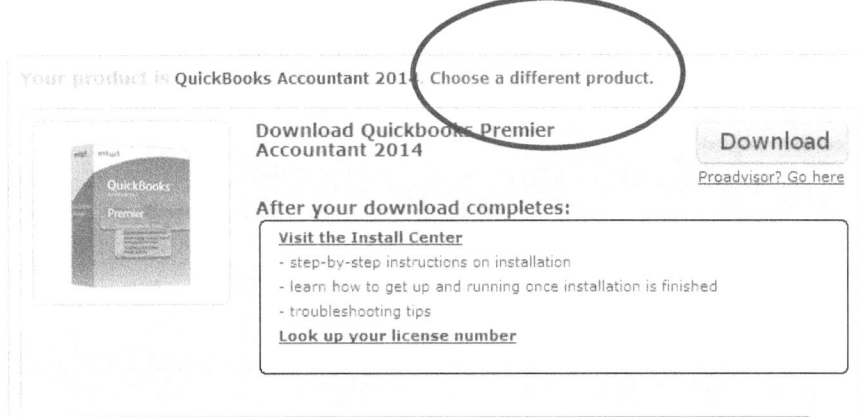

Under the Updates and downloads button, a window will open asking you "When you select a product, we can show you product-specific information." Based upon your Product Information window, complete the following steps:

1. Select your product

2. Select your version

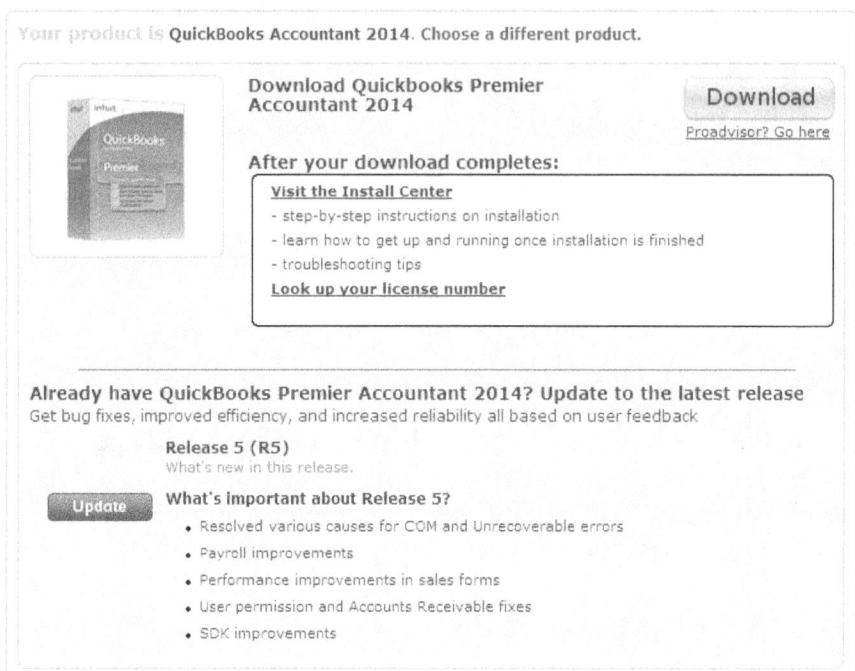

Your product is **QuickBooks Accountant 2014**. Choose a different product.

Download Quickbooks Premier Accountant 2014

Download

Proadvisor? Go here

After your download completes:

Visit the Install Center
- step-by-step instructions on installation
- learn how to get up and running once installation is finished
- troubleshooting tips

Look up your license number

Already have QuickBooks Premier Accountant 2014? Update to the latest release
Get bug fixes, improved efficiency, and increased reliability all based on user feedback

Release 5 (R5)
What's new in this release.

Update

What's important about Release 5?
- Resolved various causes for COM and Unrecoverable errors
- Payroll improvements
- Performance improvements in sales forms
- User permission and Accounts Receivable fixes
- SDK improvements

The release that is shown should be the same release number from your Product Information window. If it isn't, then you need to update your file by performing the following steps:

1. Click the Update button

2. Another window will appear at the bottom of your screen – Do you want to run or save…, for which you want to **run** if this is only on your PC or laptop. If your company file is on a server, you need to perform this update from your server, which will update the necessary file.

   Depending upon how many updates/patches you have missed, and the speed of your internet, this could take an extended period of time. When the file has been downloaded, you need to completely close the QuickBooks® software before running the patch. From there, the update performs the necessary steps to complete the process of updating your file.

If for some reason the patch times out, you may consider choosing the **save** option to which you can have the patch downloaded to your PC, such as desktop. If this option is necessary, then you still will need to continue the steps as noted above.

You may be required to restart your computer for the patch to take effect, so be aware that this is not always necessary, depending upon the patch.

After the download has been completed, when you restart your QuickBooks® program, a message will appear that you need to update your company file. You will choose **Continue** and your file will then be updated to the current patch.

Remember, the latest patch/update that's available, will cover all prior program fixes so it will not be necessary to find the other releases that may have been missed. Failing to NOT update your file can cause file issues at a later time.

Do you want to run or save **qbwebpatch.exe** (229 MB) from **http-download.intuit.com**?

This type of file could harm your computer.   Run   Save ▾   Cancel

To make sure that you have Automatic Back-Ups, choose the Help button on your Menu Bar, and when the drop-down menu appears, you are going to choose Update QuickBooks®. From there, move your cursor over the choice and right-click.

Reports   Window   Help

The following window will appear. Make sure that "Automatic Update is ON" and then choose close. If your release number doesn't match what the release number is on the QuickBooks® support site, then you can choose the Update Now button.

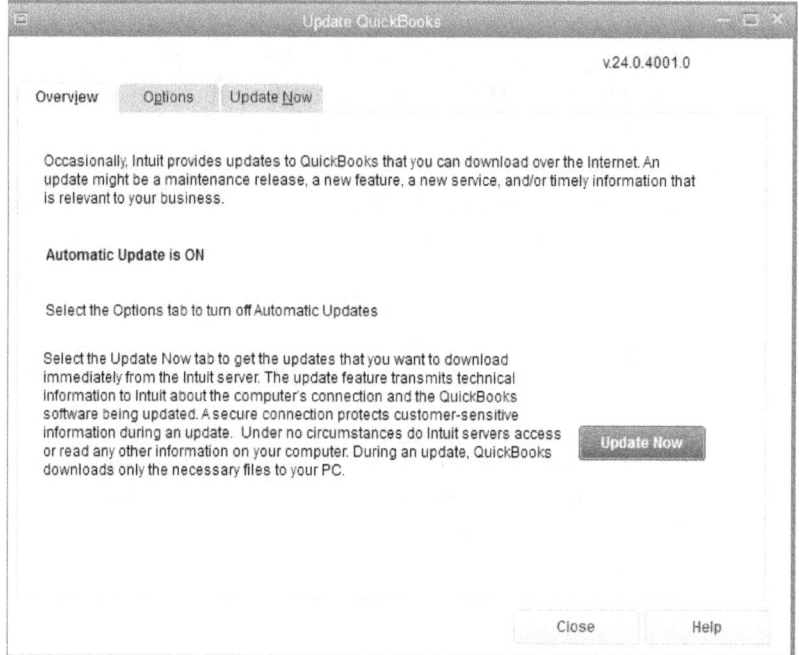

The Options tab allows you to also set your Automatic Update. The Shared Download option is if your QuickBooks® file is held on a server. If it is not, then "No" should be checked.

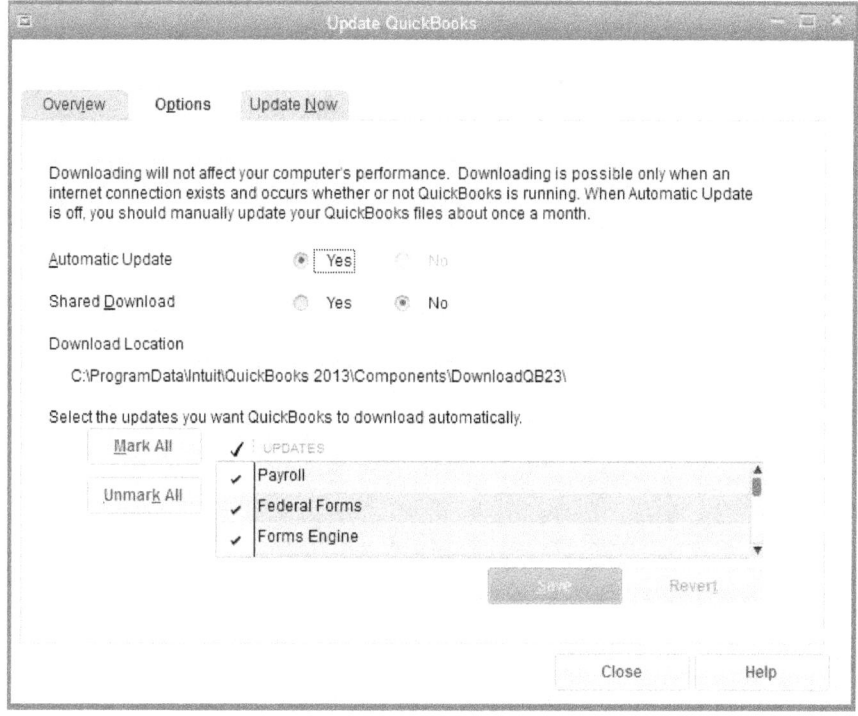

The Update Now tab shows the dates/times of your last release.

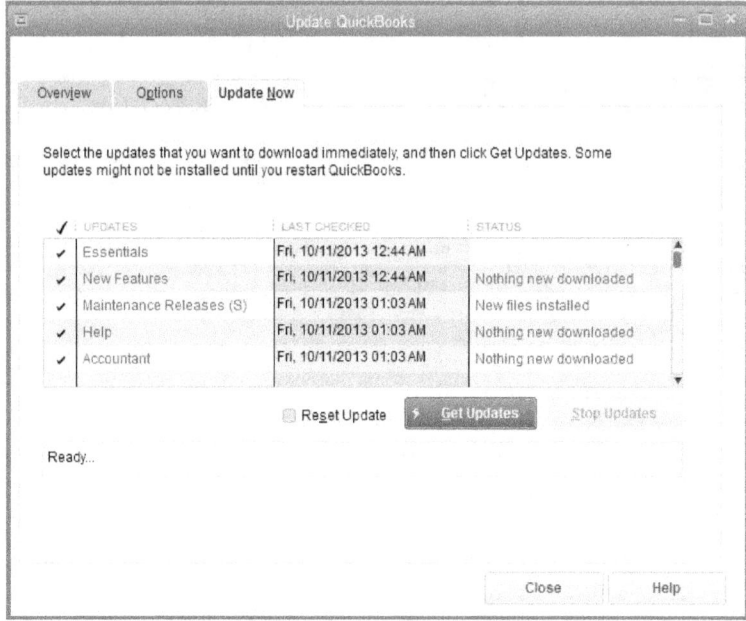

Exercises (Answer Key at the End of the Training Manual)

1.   When you are trying to determine the logistics of your company file such as year, edition, etc., what key do you choose in order to find out the information?

_____ key

2.   You must pay QuickBooks® support updates to your file?

    a. True
    b. False

3.   If you have more than one company file in QuickBooks® software, you need to download the update only one time and then opening up each company file will update each file.

    a. True
    b. False

Objective 4 – Change preferences to match company needs, including the options to structure company data for tax purposes.

As explained during Objective 1, at the top of your screen in the Menu Bar, when you move your cursor over the word Company, you will see a menu option **Company Information...** which is the sixth item down and click on it. A new window will open up, which will allow you to change all of the contact information should you need to update anything.

This information allows you to view all of your pertinent information including: version, license and product #'s, contact and legal & tax information, and any other subscriptions your company file contains. To edit the information under the Company Name section, click on the Edit button.

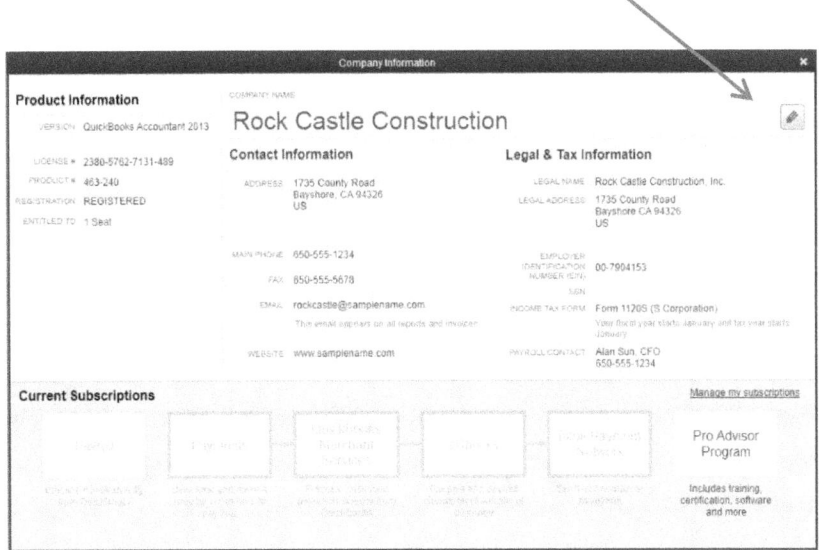

The figure below demonstrates what areas you are able to edit, and you should verify your Company Federal Employer Identification No. or Social Security Number and Payroll Tax Form Information. The Legal Name is what appears on your tax return, not on your DBA (Doing Business As) Certificate from the county clerk's office.

In the Report Information section, you will see that the Fiscal Year and Tax Year must be chosen by its first month, but it does not need to be the same month for both options. Your Tax Year can be based upon a calendar year (January – December) and your Fiscal Year can be based upon a mid-year schedule (July – June), however it's recommended that both years be equal. Income Tax Form Used section determines how the company files its taxes, but it is not necessary unless you use tax-line mapping in your Chart of Accounts.

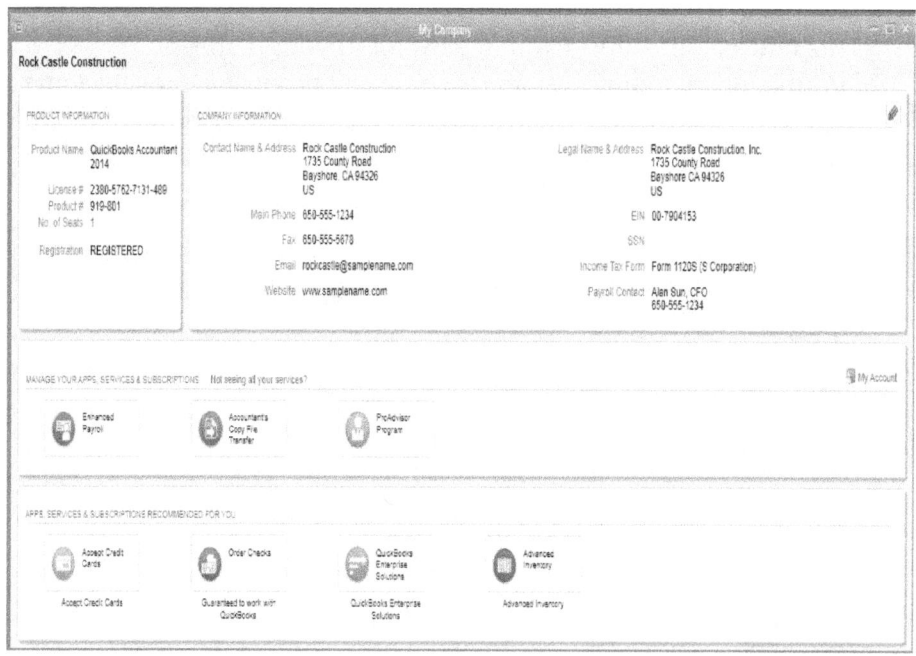

My Preferences

The first section, if there are choices to be made, is in the My Preferences tab for any users and not solely limited to the Administrator if you have multiple people set-up in your file.

Accounting: Autofill memo in general journal entry – entering memos in journal entries, it will duplicate the same memo in the corresponding entry to prevent having to retype the information

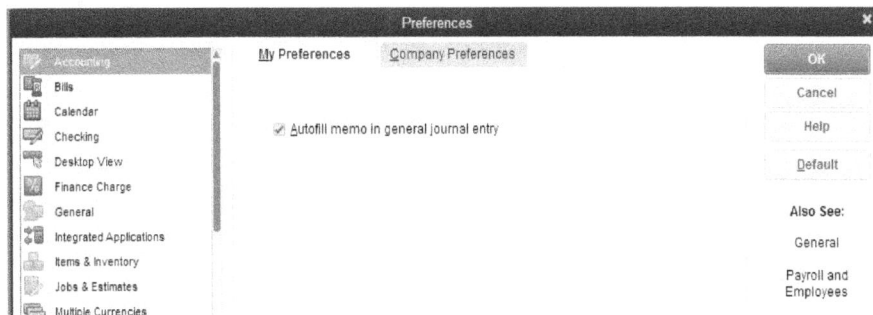

Calendar: Details the different types of views noting your tasks, to do lists, and accomplishments.

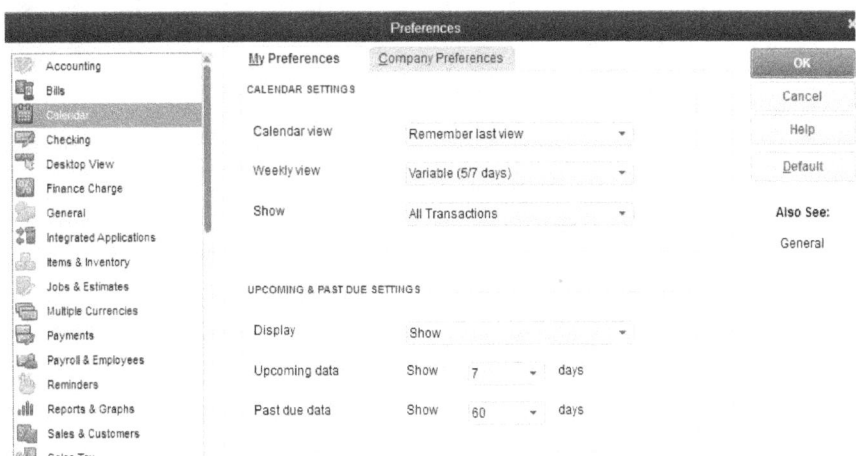

Checking: You choose if you have multiple bank savings-checking-money market accounts, what account to open for its particular corresponding task.

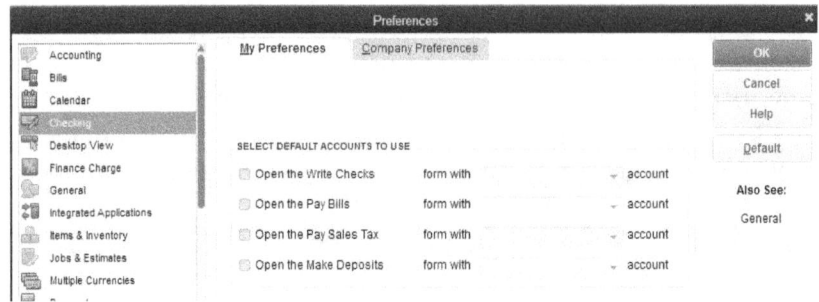

Desktop View: It's best to choose Multiple Windows in the View section, because it allows you to see various areas of your company file when working and researching different items. The Desktop section allows you to choose what you want to see when you open the company file again, as well as showing your Home Page each time you open the company. The Windows Setting helps you choose your Display and Sounds for the file.

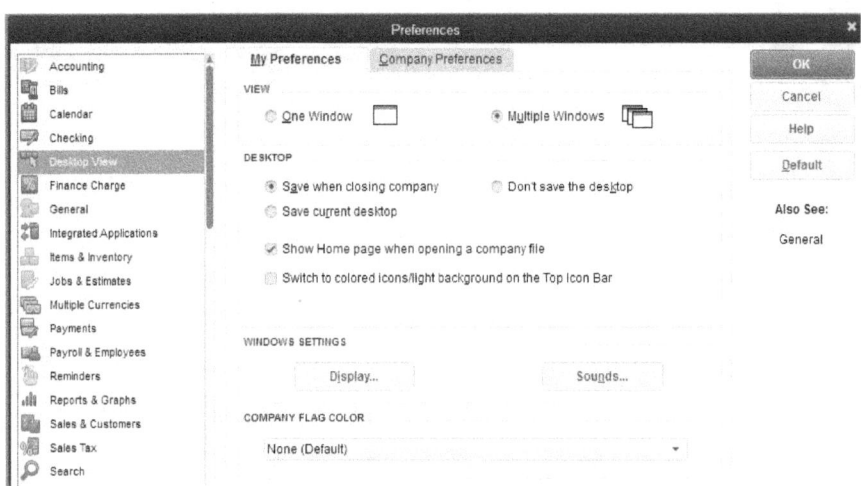

General: The first section is fairly self-explanatory, with personally recommended settings. A further explanation is added for a few of the following options:

Automatically place decimal point – when you check this box, when you enter the amount 15, it is posted as $0.15; when you leave the box unchecked, it is posted as $15.00

Pre-fill accounts for vendor based on past entries – if you have constant entries of the same type, this allows QuickBooks® to make its own determination based upon past entries for a vendor

Keep custom item information when changing item in transactions – if you choose to change the description of a List Item, then it gives you the option to either save the new description or not

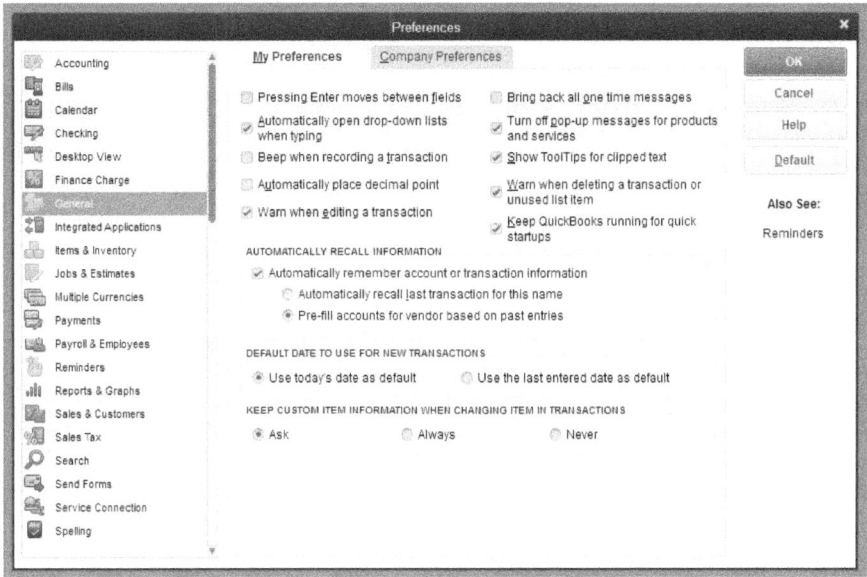

Reminders: If you use the Reminders List regarding various tasks, this option should be chosen.

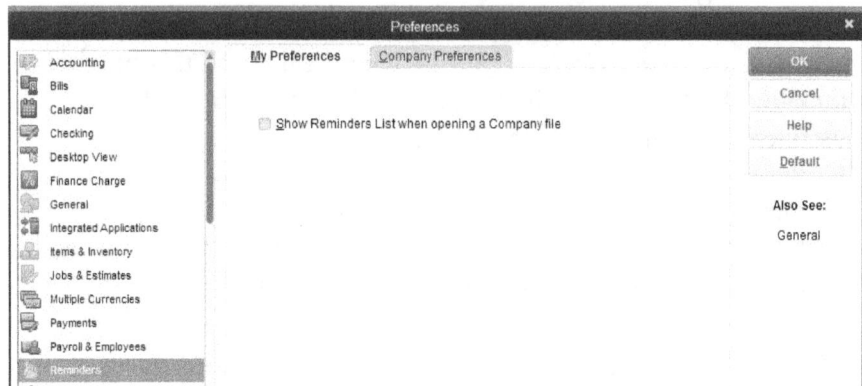

Reports & Graphs: the Refresh Automatically allows you to confirm you have updated numbers, or you can choose to refresh them yourself.

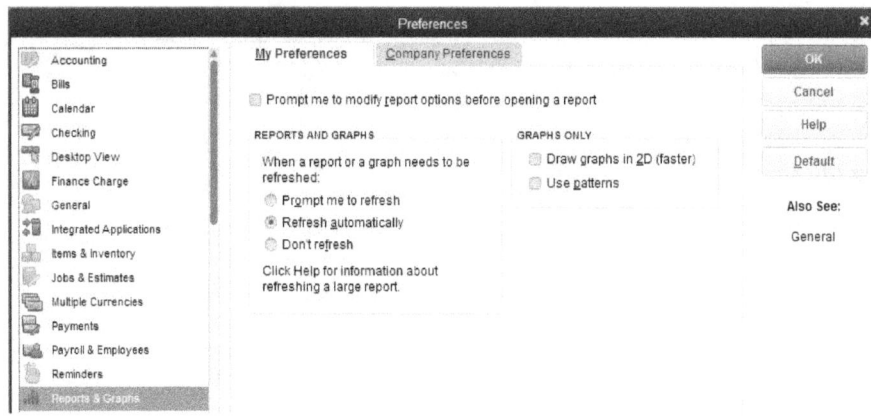

Sales & Customers: when preparing invoices, you should always choose "Ask what to do" to give you that option to determine if you want any or none from your billable options.

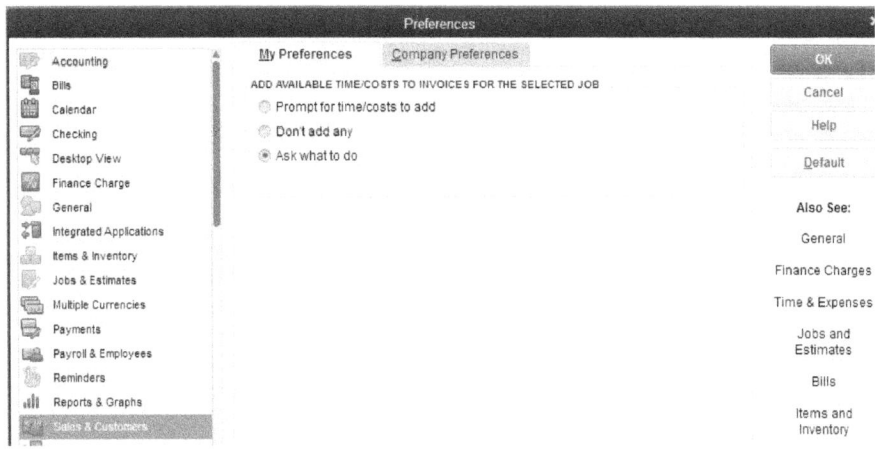

Send Forms: this option allows you to set-up e-mail preferences for invoices, purchase orders, sales orders, etc. through either Microsoft Outlook or another personal email option.

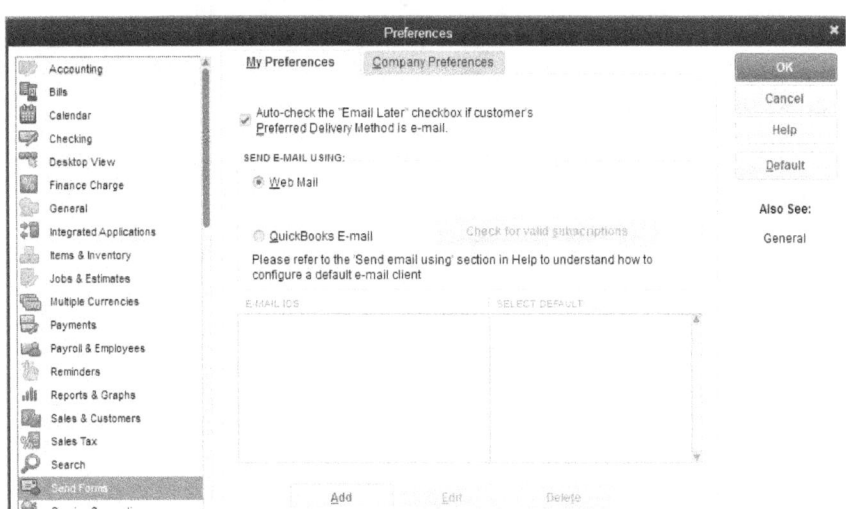

Service Connection: if you download banking information from your financial institution, then these options should be checked for access through Web Connect

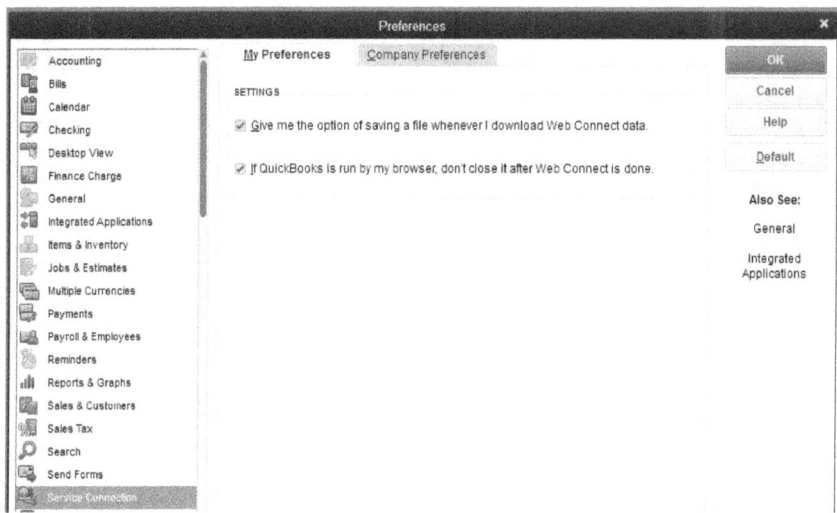

Spelling: it's recommended to always check your spelling before completion of any outside correspondence - the final section allows you to add special words, which you see the examples of QuickBooks® and TurboTax®.

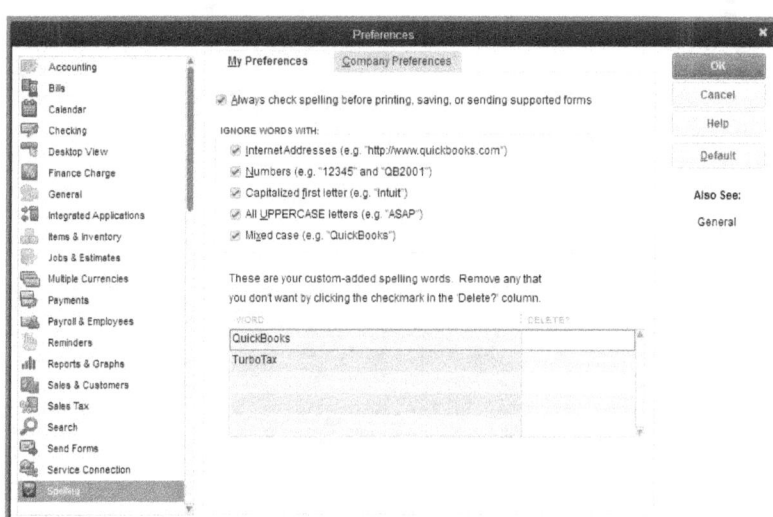

Company Preferences

When changing your company preferences, this allows **ONLY** the person who has access as the Administrator of the company file to make uniform choices for the Company but not for the User. To open the Preferences tab, choose Edit, then scroll down and choose Preferences. A Preferences window will open, with 21 areas for you to choose from. Below is a brief description of what each Preference refers to on the Company side:

Accounting: it's always recommended to choose the "Use Account Numbers" which will be outlined in the next module. The "Require Accounts" should always be checked, to prevent any transactions to be posted WITHOUT being attached to an account.

The "Show (lowest subaccount only)" is an option to allow QuickBooks® to show how your accounts are displayed, i.e. 5001:Storage Unit. If this item is not turned on, then it will display 5000:Rent:5001:Storage Unit.

Class tracking will be explained more detailed in a future module, but it allows the user(s) to set up a different set of tracking for profit and loss and/or balance sheet accounts.

Journal entry numbering is for tracking purposes and are done in sequential order. Posting transaction to the Retained Earnings account is used for accountants when closing out the books or specific accounts.

"Warning if transactions are _____ day(s) in the past" or "in the future" serves as a warning to user(s) inserting the incorrect date, however it does not prevent a date outside of that parameter from being used.

"Closing Date" allows the Administrator determine from what date, i.e. end of the month, end of the year, etc. from allowing any user to post any further transactions during the closed period. A confidential password must be used in order to prevent users from posting or making changes from closed periods, because simply setting a date does not prevent any changes from occurring. This is also a GAAP requirement upon completion of the tax returns.

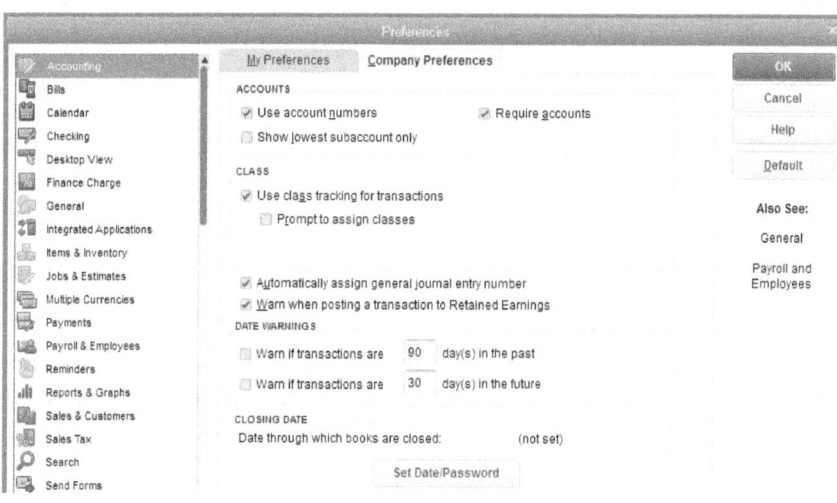

Bills:

The number "10" is set up as a default for when you enter your bills into the company file. However it's recommended to consider changing it to "0" to allow the users put in the actual bill due date because each vendor's due date will vary.

The "automatically use credits" option checked will credit any bills for which you have credits from that vendor to be applied to their current outstanding bills.

The "automatically use discounts" option checked is used for vendors who offer you an early pay discount, i.e. 2% 10 net 30 (receiving a 2% discount on your bill if it's paid within 10 days but it must be paid within 30 days). Because your vendor is taking the vendor discount as a tax deductible expense, then you, the customer, must receive that discount as taxable income.

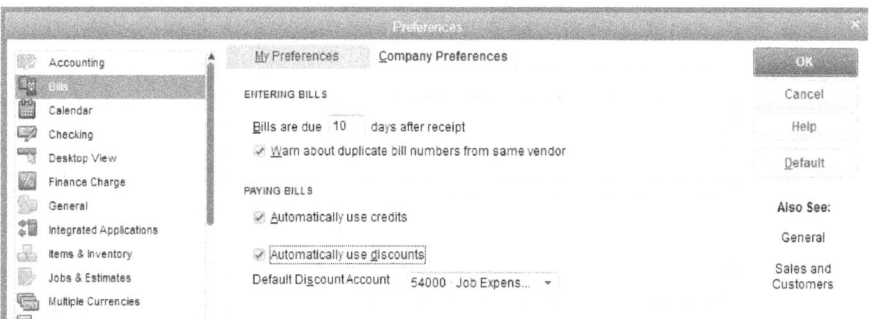

Checking:

"Print account names on voucher" allows you to print the check without detail if it is unchecked. If it is checked, all of your check detail will be printed.

"Change check date when non-cleared check is printed" will allow you to print checks with a future date if it is unchecked. If it is checked, the date the check is printed is what will appear and you will not be able to change it without unchecking this option.

"Start with payee field on check" the text cursor starts in the Bank Account field when you write checks and in the Credit Card field when you enter credit card charges. For bills, if you have more than one accounts payable account, the cursor starts in the A/P Account field; otherwise, it starts in the Vendor field if it is unchecked. If it is checked, the cursor will position itself to start typing a name into the payee field directly.

"Warn about duplicate check numbers" present a pop-up message when you enter a number which is a duplicate of one already entered, when checked.

"Autofill payee account number in check memo" populates the check with the vendor account number if one is entered in the Vendor profile.

"Open the Create Paychecks" and "Open the Pay Payroll Liabilities" account allows you to determine which account should automatically be used to pay from.

"Online Banking" will allow you to determine how you want your information to be presented when downloading your banking transactions.

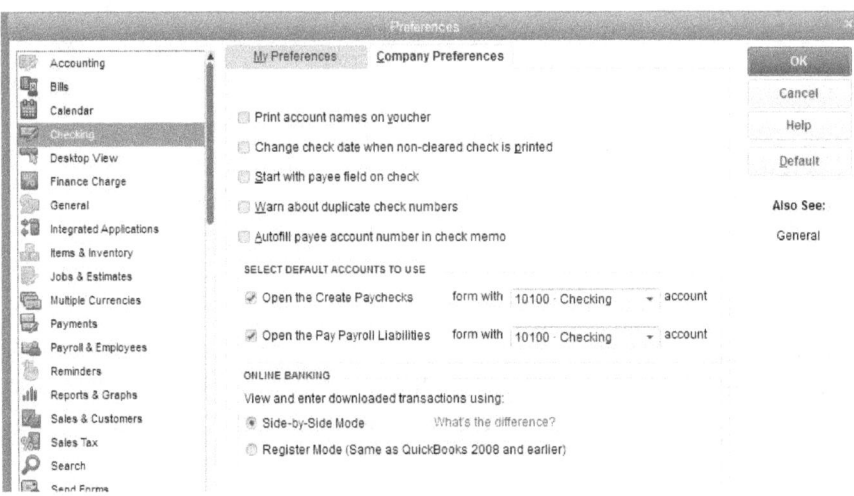

Desktop View

Presents the options of what to show on your Home Page.

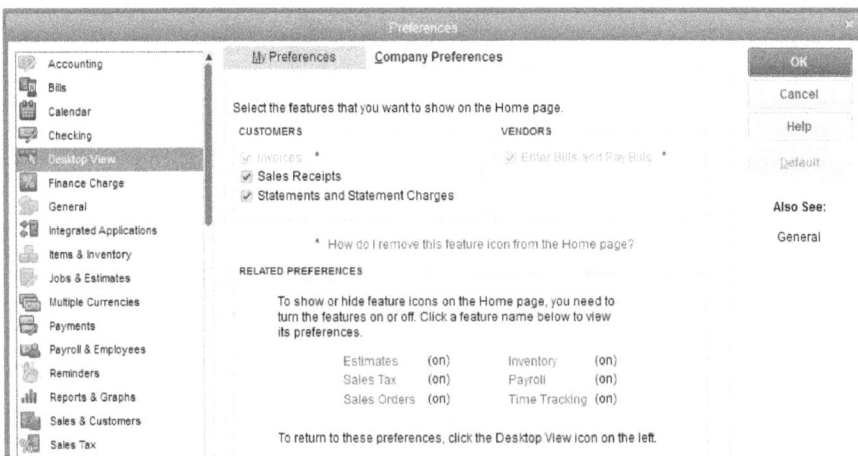

Finance Charge

Utilize for companies whose customers are required to pay finance charges based upon their written agreements and failure to pay within a timely manner. If your business chooses to set up finance charges for your customers, consult with an attorney for the proper disclosure statement and your state's allowable annual percentage rate, i.e. Texas is 18% APR.

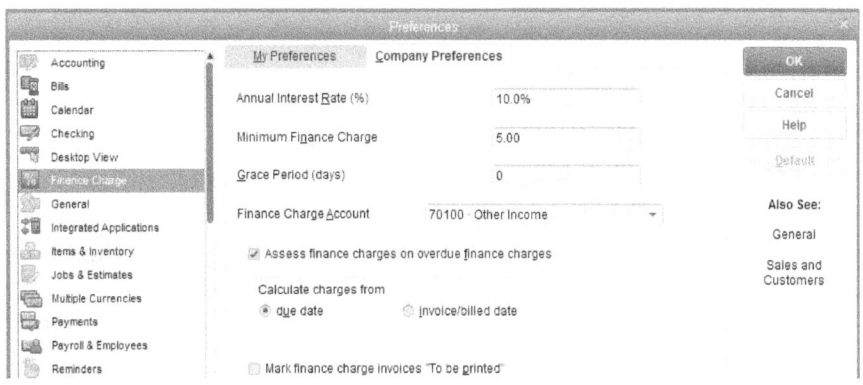

General

Shows your option of tracking your time in a decimal or minute format.

"Always show years as 4 digits (1999) is recommended for general understanding and checked.

"Never update name information when saving transactions" should be unchecked because you want your changes saved. Allowing this box to be checked can cause numerous financial errors in your reporting.

"Save transactions before printing" is a safeguard to prevent potential issues in any printed materials that do not match what is in the QuickBooks® file.

General cont.

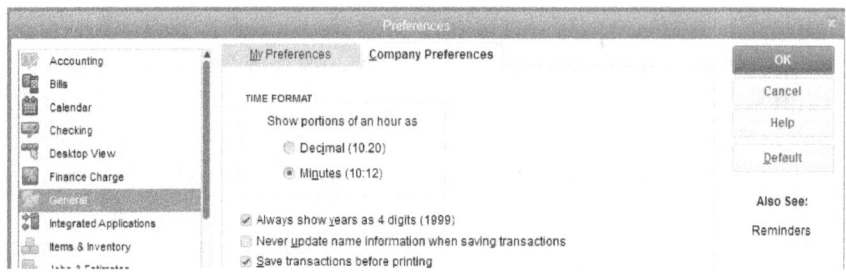

Integrated Applications

Demonstrate all applications that directly integrate and use your QuickBooks® file information from Intuit as well as other third party applications. You do have the option of either removing the application completely, refuse any applications from accessing the file, requiring your permission before any applications integrate with your file, or uncheck the application(s) you want no access to your company information.

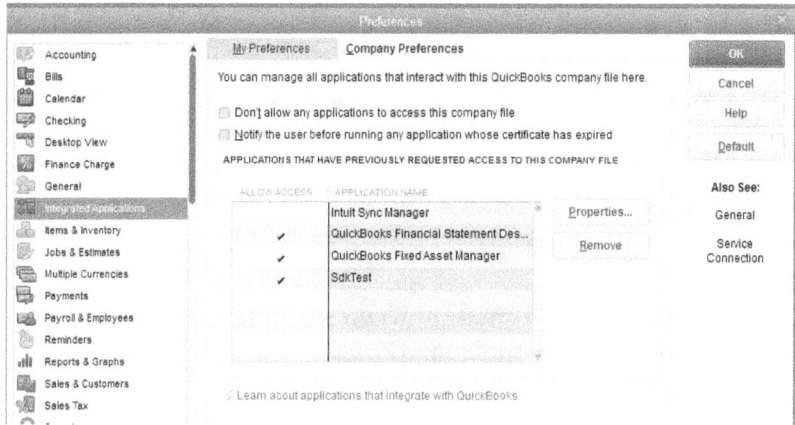

Items & Inventory

Show whether or not you use inventory and purchase order activities in your company file. If you do, then each item should be reviewed and checked appropriately. If you do not, then uncheck all of the options.

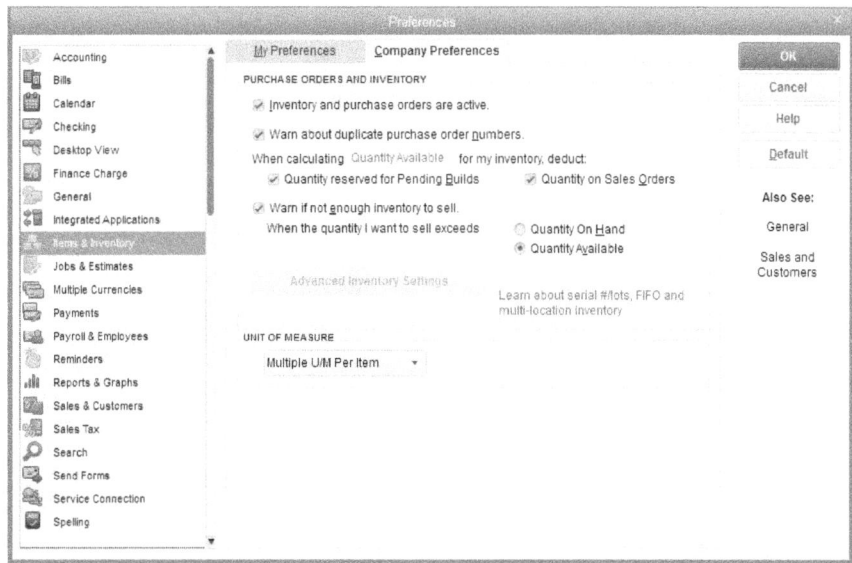

Jobs & Estimates

For those businesses that prepare proposals for customers, as well as multiple invoices for a specific project.

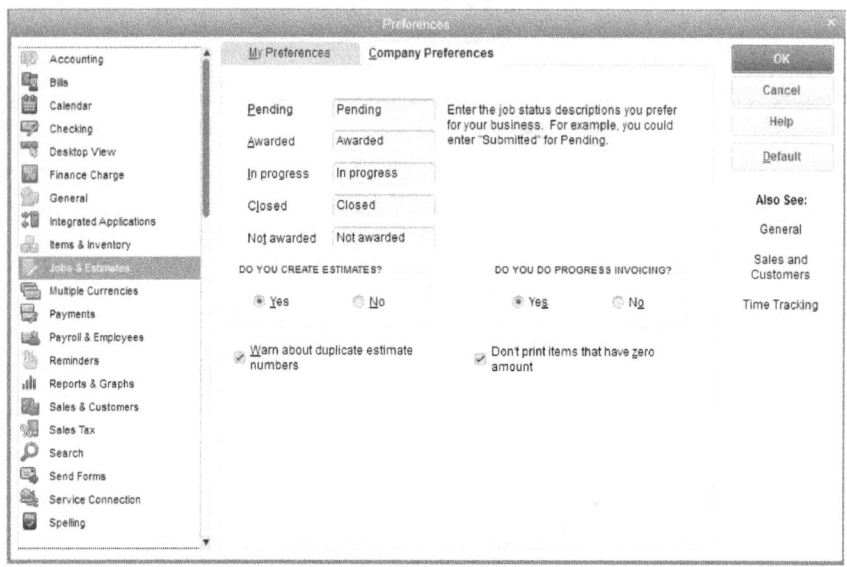

Multiple Currencies

Offers businesses the option of tracking multiple currency payments and receipts based upon that day's trading rate with U.S. Dollars being the primary currency.

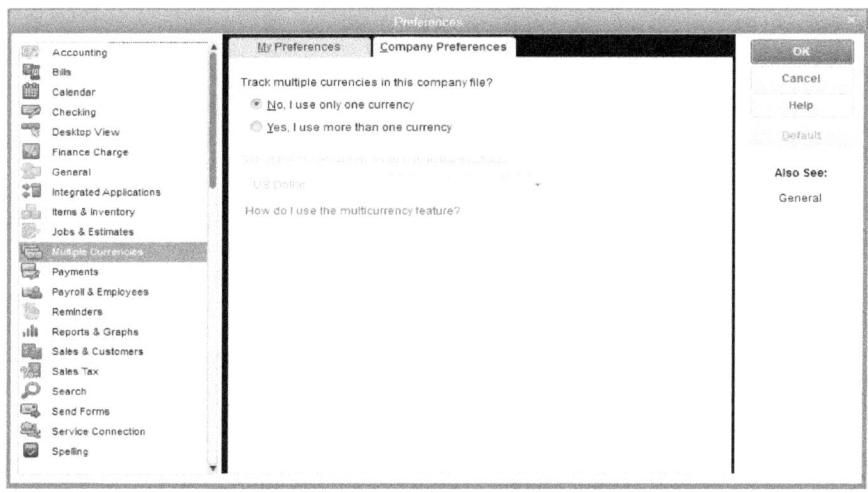

Payments

"Automatically apply payments" when checked will take each received payment and apply it to the oldest outstanding invoice.

"Automatically calculate payments" when checked will apply each received payment against the oldest invoice regardless of the amount.

"Use Undeposited Funds as a default deposit to account" collects the records of all of your received amounts into one account. From there, you will choose the payments made for that particular day and condense it into one deposit, which will allow you to perform your bank reconciliation easier.

"Intuit Payment Network" is an option that offers your customers the option of paying you directly via a bank account or credit card. Checking these options can allow you to potentially receive payments faster and maintain better cash flow instead of setting up a separate credit card merchant processing account.

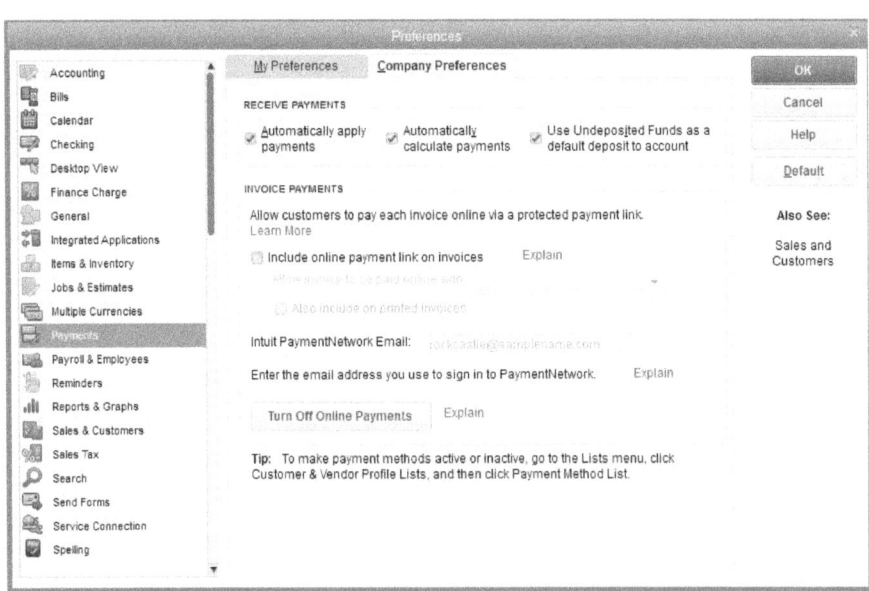

Payroll & Employees

Used if you offer payroll services through QuickBooks®. If you do not then it is not necessary to activate it and choose the "No payroll" option. If you do offer payroll services through QuickBooks®, these options will be discussed in the payroll modules.

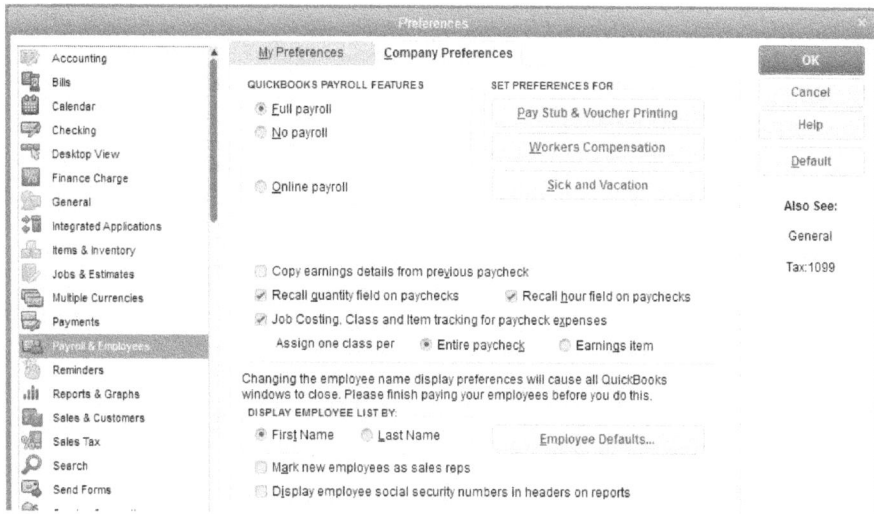

Reminders

Offers you the opportunity either set up your personal "to do list" of items and tasks, by either choosing to show it as a summary, a list, or to not set any reminders.

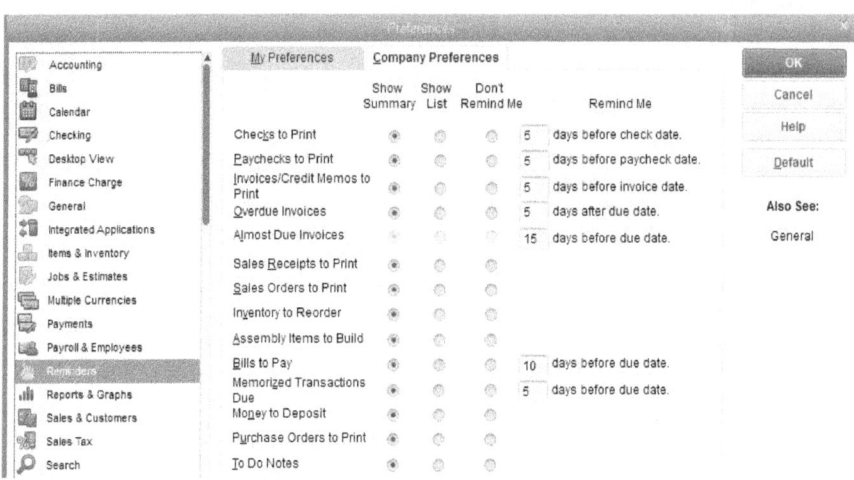

Reports & Graphs

Choose your defaults in the Reports Center. You can choose "accrual" or 'cash" based upon your tax filing status, and how your other reports are prepared based upon the accounts, items, aging status, and cash flow.

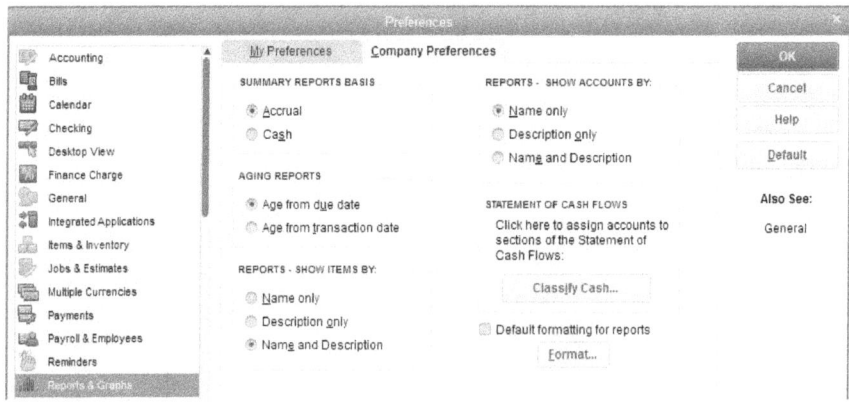

Sales & Customers

"Sales Forms" help you in utilizing your shipping method by the major carriers, i.e. UPS, Airborne, DHL, FedEx, and US Postal Office, and helps you determine the packing slip if you ship goods directly to your customers.

"Price Levels" offer you the option of setting different pricing structures for your customers.

"Sales Orders" offer you the option of keeping track of multiple orders and then you can combine those orders into a single invoice instead of utilizing multiple invoices. A sales order can also give you the option of only fulfilling a partial invoice but still tracking what other items the customer still has on order.

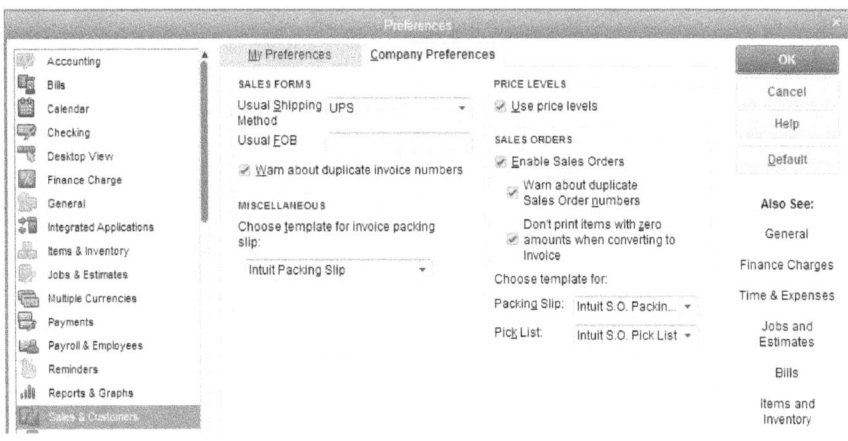

Sales Tax

To be set up if your company sells a service or product for which sales tax must be collected. This information will be described in a later module review.

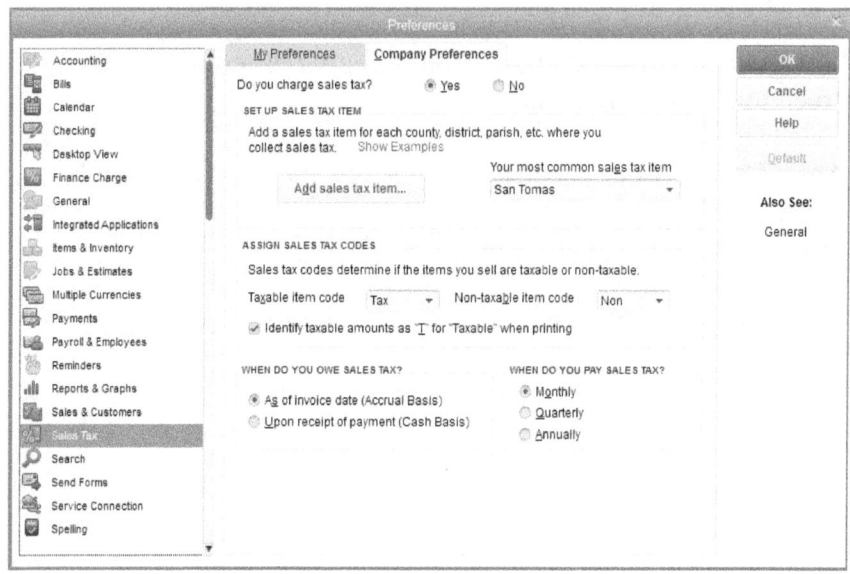

Search

Allows you to "Update automatically" when the option is checked when searching for transactions you have already entered. The time can either be set in increments of: 5 minutes, 10 minutes, 15 minutes, 30 minutes – recommended, 45 minutes, and 60 minutes.

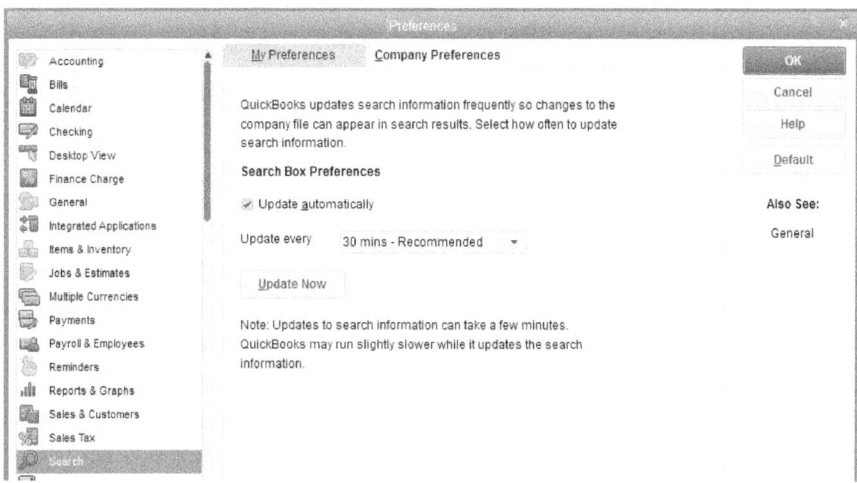

Send Forms

Allows you to set up a default e-mail message for the following forms: Invoices, Estimates, Statements, Sales Order, Sales Receipt, Credit Memo, Purchase Order, Report, Pay Stubs, Overdue Invoices, and Almost Due Invoices. Sending out these forms via e-mail, you have the option of altering the text for each recipient.

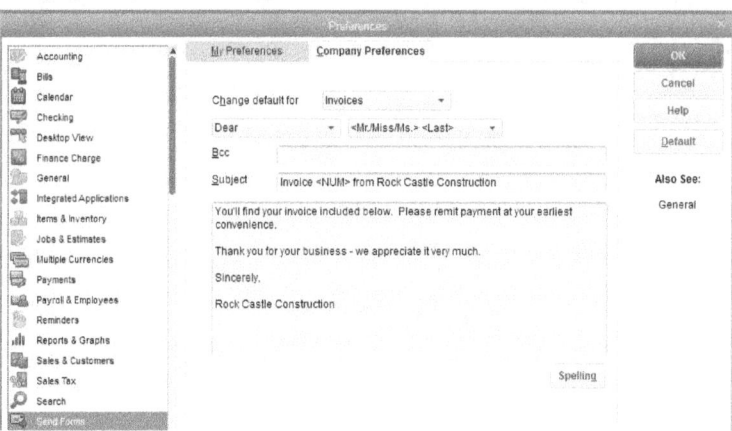

Service Connection allows you to relegate whether you allow users to e-mail information from QuickBooks® with or without a password.

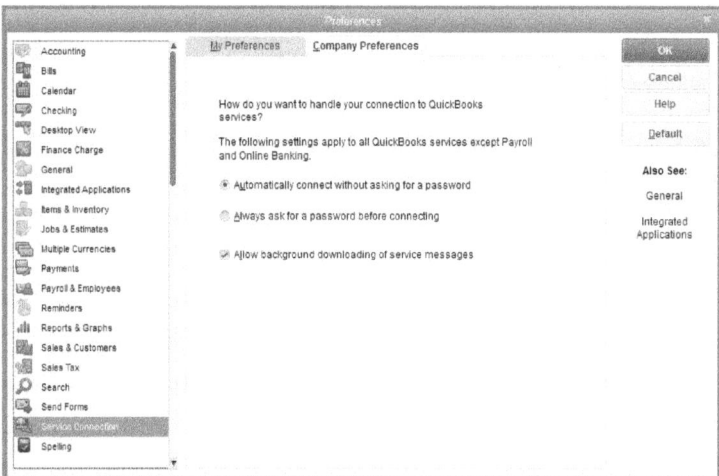

Exercises (Answer Key at the End of the Training Manual)

1.   As the individual user you do not have the option of working in the Calendar section with:

     a.   Yearly view
     b.   Show all transactions
     c.   Show upcoming data for 31 days
     d.   Past due data 14 days

2.   If you check "automatically place a decimal point" and type in the amount for fifty-three cents, it will appear as:

     a.   00.53
     b.   53.00

3.   When setting up your Sales and Customers tab, what option is not available:

     a.   Prompt for time/costs to add
     b.   Don't add any
     c.   Automatically add time/costs
     d.   Ask what to do

4.   What tab do you choose to determine your Home Page?

     _____

5.   "Change check date when non-cleared check is printed" will allow you to print checks with a future date if it is unchecked. If it is checked, the date the check is printed is what will appear and you will not be able to change it without unchecking this option.

     a.   True
     b.   False

6. "Closing Date" allows the Administrator to prevent any user to post any transactions during a closed period. A password must be used in order to prevent users from posting or making changes from closed periods because a date does not prevent any changes from occurring. This is NOT a GAAP requirement upon completion of the business tax returns.

    a. True
    b. False

7. The "Show (lowest subaccount only)" is an option to allow QuickBooks® to show how your accounts are displayed, i.e. 5001:Storage Unit. If this item is not turned on, then it will display 5000:Rent:5001:Storage Unit.

    a. True
    c. False

8. The "multiple currencies" tab is for companies who receive payments from multiple types of currency and but not pay with multiple types of currency.

    a. True
    b. False

9. "Use Undeposited Funds as a default deposit to account" collects records of all of your received amounts into one account.

    a. True
    b. False

10. "Intuit Payment Network" is an option offering your customers the option of paying you directly via a bank account or credit card.

    a. True
    b. False

Answer Key

<u>Objective 1</u>

1.   Legal Name
           Zip Code
           Phone

2.   W-9
           Payroll
           Sales Tax
           Income Tax Return

<u>Objective 2</u>

1.   70%

2.   3
           Complete

<u>Objective 3</u>

1.   F2

2.   False

3.   True

<u>Objective 4</u>

1.	Yearly view	6.	False
2.	00.53	7.	True
3.	Automatically add time/costs	8.	False
4.	Desktop View	9.	True
5.	True	10.	True